LADY OTTOLINE'S ALBUM

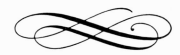

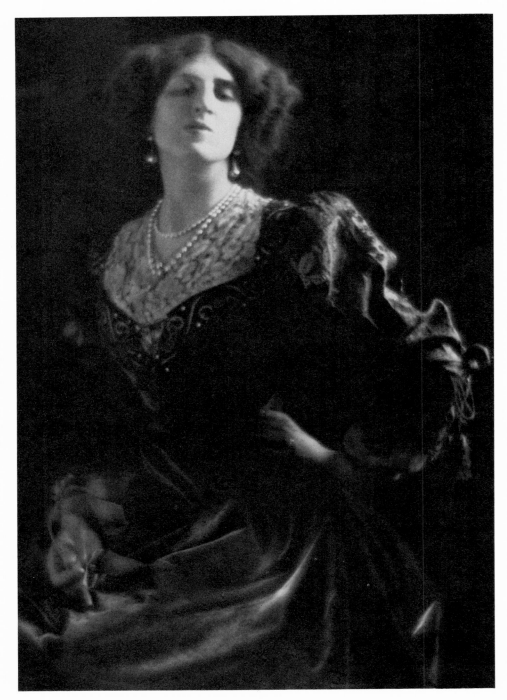

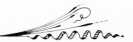

LADY OTTOLINE'S ALBUM

Snapshots and portraits of her famous contemporaries

(and of herself), photographed for the most part by

LADY OTTOLINE MORRELL

From the collection of her daughter,
JULIAN VINOGRADOFF

With an Introduction by
LORD DAVID CECIL

Edited by
CAROLYN G. HEILBRUN

MICHAEL JOSEPH – LONDON

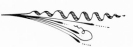

First published in Great Britain by
MICHAEL JOSEPH LIMITED
52 Bedford Square, London W.C.1
1976

Since this page cannot legibly accommodate all permissions acknowledgments,
they may be found on page 116.

The frontispiece photograph of Lady Ottoline Morrell is by Baron de Meyer.

ISBN 0 7181 1483 3

Printed and bound in the United States of America

CONTENTS

FOREWORD

All these photographs were taken by my mother, with the exception of the very early ones, dating from about 1902 to 1910, which were taken by my father. (Of course the ones in which my mother herself appears must have been taken by someone else.) She worked with a variety of cameras, and was constantly changing them with dealers in London. I think the greatest number of pictures were taken with a Rolliflex, which she found easiest to focus. She always used the finest makes of German cameras, which were then the best as Japanese cameras had not become known, and neither of course had colour photography. My mother was a very lavish photographer; she took any number of pictures, regardless of expense, and then selected the ones she liked most. She started the pictures at Garsington with a very small camera—I think it was called a Vest Pocket Kodak—which is responsible for the tiny pictures, taken in 1915 or 1916. She soon abandoned this.

It is startling to note that none of the indoor pictures was taken with flash-lights, if indeed these were known then. She posed her subjects close to the windows, and managed to get very successful results.

The photographs were stuck into a series of albums—twelve in all, bound in white vellum with vellum ties—and pasted on dark blue paper. I have put a short index on the outside of each album, giving the names of the celebrities inside, because I got very tired over the years searching for them in the twelve volumes. Of course, most of them appear in several volumes. The photographs get clearer and better the more recently they were taken and the ones shot in 1936 and 1937 are simply excellent in sharpness and brilliance. Mother used first-class London firms to do her developing and printing. She was always taking snapshots of her favourite subjects—Bertie Russell, Aldous Huxley, Virginia Woolf, W. B. Yeats, Siegfried Sassoon, and others, among them the many undergraduates who came out to see us. She was particularly fond of taking Lytton Strachey and André Gide. My main memory of her at weekends is with a camera held to her left eye, stalking her subjects. I suppose they knew very well that they were being taken.

—JULIAN MORRELL VINOGRADOFF

LADY OTTOLINE'S ALBUM

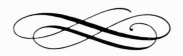

INTRODUCTION
by Lord David Cecil

This volume presents a pictorial record of Lady Ottoline Morrell and the circle of which she was the centre and creator. As such, it is a document of historic importance. For this circle was something unique in the social history of twentieth-century England.

So also was Lady Ottoline. Born in 1872, she was the daughter of General Arthur Cavendish Bentinck and his wife, Lady Bolsover. Her half-brother succeeded to the Dukedom of Portland and she and her mother migrated to the family seat of Welbeck. The last Duke had been eccentric. This showed in his house, which consisted largely of huge underground rooms and pink and gold apartments for guests, empty but for an open water closet in the corner. Here Lady Ottoline grew up. Before she was eighteen she had showed herself utterly unlike the conventional young lady, possessed of a strange majestic beauty and an extravagance of imaginative temperament that craved to lose itself in spiritual rapture. "Life," she once wrote, "lived on the same plane as poetry and as music, is my distinctive desire and standard. It is the failure to accomplish this which makes me discontented with myself." She could not accomplish it as a Victorian debutante and sought other modes of living. First she plunged into evangelical religion and held prayer-meetings for her mother's footmen. Though the footmen could not but like her, they found the prayer-meetings embarrassing. Nor did they satisfy Lady Ottoline's longings. She next persuaded her relations—who found her an uncomfortable element in their homes—to let her travel. With a friend and a governess she spent months abroad, especially in Italy, soaking herself in the beauties of art and nature, and there she fell in love with Dr. Axel Munthe. This romance came to nothing. Lady Ottoline now tried the life of study: first at the University of St. Andrew's and then at Oxford. It was now that she met and married Philip Morrell. They were to have two children, of which only one, a daughter called Julian, lived to grow up. Philip Morrell was the son of an Oxford legal family, and picturesquely handsome in a high-nosed Regency style with a taste for the arts and left-wing Liberal ideals. This

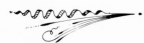
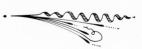

marriage, though like everything else in Lady Ottoline's life it was to have its dramas, was close and devoted. Morrell shared her artistic tastes—together they travelled, visited galleries, and attended concerts—while she, to the horror of her family, threw herself into helping him in his career as a Liberal Member of Parliament. She was never a politician, however; and her chief energies were given to her private life. She was still primarily concerned to achieve an existence "lived on the same plane as poetry and as music" and she worked to surround herself with people who could assist her in this enterprise. It was now that her circle began to form itself, mainly at their house in London, No. 44 Bedford Square. As might be expected, this circle included few if any persons from the blue-blooded and Philistine world in which she had been brought up; and consisted of artists, writers, and thinkers, sprung from every kind of place and background, many of them, like herself, in rebellion against the conventions of whatever world they might happen to have been born into. Lady Ottoline had an instinctive eye for quality in human beings and the circle was over the years to be ornamented by many famous names; Bertrand Russell, W. B. Yeats, D. H. Lawrence, T. S. Eliot, Katherine Mansfield, Lytton Strachey, Virginia Woolf, Augustus John, Henry Lamb, Mark Gertler, Aldous and Julian Huxley, Stanley and Gilbert Spencer, E. M. Forster, Elizabeth Bowen, Duncan Grant, Walter de la Mare—all these were among her friends.

Some of them became more than friends. Lady Ottoline was a passionate and possessive character; and, for her, life lived on the same plane as poetry and as music meant life lived on an emotional plane dangerously high. One friendship, that with Bertrand Russell, turned into a stormy love affair; and, even when her friendships did not actually involve love, they tended to get overheated to a point which ended in an explosion, followed by a breach. However, while they lasted, both love affairs and friendships were rapturous and fruitful. Lady Ottoline's spirit and sympathy stimulated the creative activities of her protégés. She also assisted them by buying their works and gave them practical help later by having them to stay for long periods at her home in the country.

For in 1913 the Morrells decided to move from London to Garsington Manor near Oxford. They did not, however, get possession of it till 1915. By this time the First World War had been going for a year. This had made a great change in their life; for they were militant pacifists openly opposed to the war. Indeed Philip Morrell had been one of the few Members of Parliament to make a

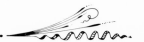

speech against it in the crucial Parliamentary debate which decided that England should fight. As a result of their views, the Morrells found themselves cut off from the majority of their countrymen and Garsington became a sort of home of refuge for those of their friends who shared their unpopular views. Some of these were conscientious objectors ordered to do agricultural work. Philip Morrell, in order to occupy himself in the country, had taken up farming: he was therefore able to employ them as workers on his farm. The natives of Garsington watched with surprise and amusement the figures of fastidious littérateurs nervously and ineffectively trying to herd sheep or drive unwilling cows through a gate.

The end of the war saw the revival of Lady Ottoline's circle, this time at Garsington. Old friends came back and she made some new ones, notably Siegfried Sassoon, whose protests against the war, when he was in the army, had stirred her admiration. There were other new friends too from Oxford University, dons and undergraduates who shared her interests; L. P. Hartley, Edward Sackville-West, Peter Quennell, Maurice Bowra are among the names that spring to my mind. They came mostly on Sunday afternoons to meet the visitors from elsewhere who came to spend the weekend, though Lady Ottoline was very likely also to have some impecunious artist or writer staying in the house for a longer visit.

In 1928 came once more a change; the Morrells decided to go back to London. There were various reasons for this. They were not rich people by the standards of their time and position, and they found Garsington life too expensive, especially as Philip, no farmer by education, lost money on his farm. Further, both he and Lady Ottoline were getting older and they wanted to live in a smaller, quieter way. Finally, Garsington for Lady Ottoline had come to be associated with some distressing memories; memories of the painful ending of some of her valued friendships. In particular, D. H. Lawrence and Aldous Huxley, two men she had been particularly fond of, had repaid her affection by publishing books, *Women in Love* and *Crome Yellow*, which portrayed her and life at her home in unflattering terms. The result had been a quarrel with both; and though later she was to be reconciled to them, they never again became the friends they had been before. Meanwhile she connected them with Garsington and liked it less in consequence.

In 1928 the Morrells settled in London at No. 10 Gower Street and Lady

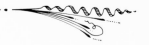

Ottoline entered on what was to be the final phase of her life. It was to be a less dramatic phase. The world had changed and she was a woman over fifty with a married daughter. But her aims and mode of living remained basically the same. Thursdays at teatime were times for gatherings (in winter by fireside, in summer under the garden trees) of old friends and new—still chosen as likely to contribute to the life lived on the plane of poetry and of music, though the music was gentler and the poetry less impassioned than that which had echoed so resoundingly through the halls of Garsington during the hey-day of her life there.

Physical causes also helped to keep things quieter. Lady Ottoline's health had never been good. Now it grew worse and she also began to suffer from deafness. Soon came an additional affliction in the shape of necrosis of the jaw. This led to a very serious operation. Lady Ottoline recovered from this but was noticeably weaker. Her weakness increased, her health declined; she died in 1938 at the age of sixty-six.

Myself, I only got to know her in 1921 after the most dramatic phases of her life were over. But her personality was still sensational. If I remember rightly, the first time I saw her was on a summer morning in Oxford High Street. I was standing on the steps of the Examination Schools: the usual crowd was jostling on the pavement, the women in the fashion of that period dressed mostly in straight flat shortish garments, which concealed the figure but revealed the legs, and wearing hats like inverted flower pots that cast a shadow over their faces, so that it was hard to tell one from another. Then, sailing slowly through the crowd, which made way for her with much staring and whispering, a figure caught my eye—stately, upright, very tall and clad in a dress of canary-coloured silk, shaped closely to her bosom and waist, and then spreading out in long full skirts that swept the pavement. On her rust-coloured hair she wore a wide-brimmed hat of royal blue trimmed with curling ostrich feathers also of royal blue. She moved with heavily powdered countenance raised a little up, as if lost in some brooding dream, and oblivious of the stir she was creating. "It is Lady Ottoline Morrell," said a voice near me.

Soon afterwards I met her in the room of Morven Bentinck, a fellow undergraduate of mine and her nephew. Close to, she looked even more startling than at a distance. Lady Ottoline was the only person I have ever seen who could

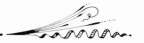

look, at one and the same moment, beautiful and what I can only call grotesque. Henry James once said of her: "She is like some gorgeous heraldic creature—a Gryphon perhaps or a Dragon Volant!" Her appearance ran to extremes: her figure was magnificent, so was her noble forehead and her deep-set sombre eyes. But beneath them jutted strangely out a long equine jaw and heavy mouth which from time to time opened to reveal large equine teeth. Her clothes, too, from which exhaled a musky delicate scent, blended unexpected characteristics. They looked splendid and picturesque but not fresh or new. One would hardly have been surprised to learn that the dress she was wearing had belonged to Queen Elizabeth the First; and Queen Elizabeth's, too, might have been the ropes of irregular pearls twisted round her neck.

Meanwhile their wearer was asking me, in curious slow sing-song tones that rose up and down the scale from treble to baritone, whether I would come out to Garsington on the following Sunday. I had already heard of Garsington as a place where one met distinguished artists and writers. At the age of nineteen I longed passionately to meet such people; I also longed to see more of Lady Ottoline. I accepted.

I was not disappointed. The artists and writers were there—Yeats, I think, and Mark Gertler and Siegfried Sassoon; and of course Lady Ottoline. She was more impressive than ever in her own setting. Looking back over the past I think that Garsington Manor was the most beautiful house I have ever seen— or I should rather say the most beautiful "modern" house; for though it had been built in the time of James I, Lady Ottoline and Philip Morrell, together— for both were responsible for the decoration—had combined to create out of it a work of original imaginative art, revealing a highly individual taste which extended to every detail of its furnishings down to the very writing paper and the matchboxes. In particular I recall a matchbox contrived out of an antique Dutch box of engraved steel and copper.

It was, I suppose, an incorrect use for an antique Dutch box; but the Morrells did not go in for correctness. There was no question, for instance, of their leaving the panelled walls a sober brown according to the orthodox taste of the time. On the contrary they had them painted all over in colours rich and subtle and on them hung gleaming mirrors and also pictures by contemporary artists; pensive elegant ladies by Conder, pensive heroic-looking peasant women by Henry Lamb and Augustus John. They were romantic pictures: Lady Ottoline's

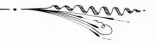

taste was intensely romantic. That is why, in spite of its originality, it harmonized with the old romantic Jacobean house. Romantically the rooms rise through the mists of memory to confront my mental eye, all smelling faintly and delicately of Lady Ottoline's scent mingled with that of the incense she liked to burn over the wood fire: the Venetian-red drawing room, with the oranges stuck with cloves on the mantelpiece; the hall of delicate dove-grey; and Lady Ottoline's little sitting room upstairs, book-lined and with woodwork and wainscot painted a dim peacock-green with hints of gold on the mouldings and with mullioned latticed windows framed with pale honey-hued curtains.

The curtains were faded and the gilt a little rubbed. But this was not out of keeping with the room; nor with the rest of the house either. Like Lady Otto-line's clothes, her house did not go in for looking spick-and-span and new. It was beautiful and a little shabby; and the shabbiness enhanced the beauty. It made it seem lived-in—and ancient and dreamlike—and it removed from it the least trace of the interior decorator's exhibition piece or of the rich man's toy. Indeed, as I have said, the Morrells were not rich; and, by the standards of their day and station in life, did not live richly. They had few servants, their food was good but simple; there was not a great deal to drink.

Moreover, beauty had sometimes been achieved at the expense of *conforts modernes*. The garden was as romantically beautiful as the house, with its grassy terrace leading down to a pool that reflected yews and an ilex tree and statues brought from Italy. It was said that if the Morrells had to choose between adding a bathroom to their house or a statue to their garden they would choose the statue. If this was true, they were, I thought, to be congratulated. Lady Ottoline clearly had got her priorities right.

Altogether, I was captivated alike by the house and by its châtelaine. From that time on I went to Garsington as often as I got the chance, both at weekends, when there were a lot of visitors there, and in the week, when there were few or none. After Lady Ottoline had gone to London I went to see her there when I had the opportunity. I recognized that social life at her house was, as I have said, something unique.

Posterity, to judge by references to that era, has not always realized this. People write of Lady Ottoline as a fashionable lion-huntress, a member of the great world who asked famous people to her house because they were famous. She was nothing of the kind. For one thing, though she had been born in the

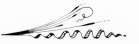

great world, she had left it early and during the First War had lived in open opposition to it. In later life, it is true, she did pick up old threads, saw more of her family and the society they lived in. But she never returned to live in it. Her closest friends still belonged to the very different society she had found for herself; so did those persons who played the most important parts in her life. The only exception was Bertrand Russell, and he, like her, was an aristocrat who had deliberately broken with the world into which they had both been born.

How far she had moved from it was comically apparent on the occasions when she did chance to come into contact with conventional society. By 1920 Garsington had become famous as a beautiful house frequented by the distinguished and the eccentric; with the result that people wanted to visit it. Now and again, especially on summer Sunday afternoons, its lawns would be invaded by persons who had contrived to get introductions to Lady Ottoline. Sober visitors from American universities, parties from fashionable country houses in the neighbourhood, they would appear in the garden, looking confident enough. But their confidence ebbed visibly as they caught sight of the shaggy-headed and bohemian-looking company assembled on its lawns. Nor was it restored when there rose from among these intimidating groups the grand and fantastic figure of their hostess. Graciously she greeted them; but her appearance, her voice and manner of speech, were so different from anything they were accustomed to that she only made them ill at ease; all the more because the rest of her guests were liable to stare at them for a moment with a concentrated unsmiling curiosity and then turn silently away.

Different were occasional invasions from The Wharf, Sutton County, the home of Lord and Lady Oxford. Margot, Lady Oxford, was as unusual as Lady Ottoline but in a different way, a child of nature—or more precisely an *enfant terrible* of nature—vivid, dominating, restless, alarmingly outspoken. She had no circle, but each weekend collected at her home a heterogeneous assembly of persons ranging from international tycoons and foreign ambassadors to out-of-work actors and schoolboys on holiday who had nothing in common with each other and whom often she hardly knew herself. Having got them to her house, she was apt to leave them to their own devices while she played bridge; but sometimes by way of entertaining them she swept them over to Garsington in a fleet of cars. No question of shyness here! These invasions were in the nature of daylight raids by an up-to-date warplane; Margot swooping down to drop

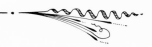

some devastating missile of outspoken criticism on Lady Ottoline's clothes, her guests, and her daughter's looks and then, in a flash, streaking up into the sky and away. Lord Oxford wandered behind her looking like a benevolent and bibulous Oliver Cromwell: he had known the Morrells in their political days and diffused a more soothing atmosphere than did his mercurial wife. In fact he did not need to; it took more than Lady Oxford to disconcert Lady Ottoline. She, while the visit lasted, maintained an air of patrician detachment and an enigmatic gleam in her strange eyes. After it was over she settled back with relief to enjoy the more congenial company of her own guests.

If Lady Ottoline did not live in the great world, neither could she be called a lion-huntress. Apart from anything else few of her friends were lions when she got to know them: Lytton Strachey and Aldous Huxley, for instance, were both undergraduates. She picked them out, according to her custom, because she thought they could contribute to the life of the spirit to which she aspired. Many of her protégés often did become famous later: but if they did not it made no difference to her interest in and affection for them. Some of the faces regularly seen at Garsington and Gower Street were not the faces of lions nor of people who had any prospect of becoming lions.

Further, the lions themselves were not treated as such, not exhibited before an admiring world for the glory of their hostess. I noticed this on my first visit. The lions were there all right—Yeats, Sassoon, and the rest—but they were not on show, not caged. Rather I saw them in their natural haunts, relaxed, un-observed, at play; or, if they wanted to work, free to go and do so. As for Lady Ottoline, she seemed to be one of them. This, above all, was what made her relation to her guests different from that of the fashionable hostesses to whom she is sometimes compared. So far from being a lion-huntress, she was a lion herself, a creative artist of the private life, whose imagination expressed itself in the clothes she wore, the rooms she sat in, the social life that took place there, and, more than anything, in herself. In the company of her distinguished friends she seemed of their spiritual kin, and in force and originality of personality wholly their equal. One looked at her and listened to her and remembered her as much as them.

Not that she sought to dominate the conversation; she asked questions rather than made statements. All the same it was she who set the talk going, stimulated others to contribute to it, guided its course. She it was who con-

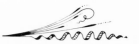

ducted the conversational orchestra and made it play her tune, the tune of her personality.

This personality was as arresting and individual as her clothes. Like them, she did not seem to belong to the twentieth century. I find myself frequently using the word "Elizabethan" to describe her; for she seemed built on the Elizabethan scale with Elizabethan grandeur, imagination, and passion. Moreover, she blended, in the Elizabethan fashion, the spiritual and the earthy. The spiritual element was very noticeable. Though she had moved a long way from the young girl who had held prayer-meetings for the footmen at Welbeck, she had remained in some way of her own profoundly religious. She responded intensely to every kind of mystical and visionary art; her talk often soared upwards in mysterious fanciful flights bewildering to people today but likely to have been, I suspect, less so to people in the days of Shakespeare.

But her response—sensual, full-blooded, unbridled—to the beautiful was also of the age of Shakespeare; so too, and unexpectedly, was a streak of robust and rollicking Shakespearian humour. There was nothing precious or genteel about Lady Ottoline. She was an early enthusiast for the first Charlie Chaplin films; she delighted in fairs and music halls and slapstick comedy. Nor did she mind a little vulgarity, just as she did not mind a little dust and dirt. A friend of hers was startled once to see her pick up a bun from the dusty floor and eat it with zest. "I love buns off the floor," she said with a sort of stately mischievous glee. An infectious glee was one of her agreeable qualities; mischief was another. I was sometimes amused to note that the persons who made fun of her seemed unaware of what excellent fun she could make of them. It was a further paradox of her nature that she often alternated the flights of her high-flown romanticism with flashes of impish satire.

Of such varied and incongruous ingredients was compounded the personality that reigned over the social scene at Garsington and Gower Street. It was a varied scene. Within the limits of her interests, Lady Ottoline's circle was very diverse. Not only was she willing to try out persons on the face of it alien to her outlook—I remember meeting H. G. Wells at her house, though only once—but even those with whom she found herself in sympathy and who came often could be very unlike each other. Apparently it took all sorts to promote the good life of the spirit as she conceived it. The Bloomsbury representatives, for

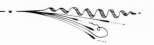

instance, in the persons of Lytton Strachey and Virginia Woolf, were wonderfully different from the Celtic movement as personified by Yeats and James Stephens: Bloomsbury fastidious, rational, and awkwardly silent with strangers, the Celts flamboyant, irrational, and ready to perorate eloquently to anyone who would listen to them about leprechauns and the Mystic Rose and Lady Gregory.

The Garsington poets too presented a contrast to each other, especially to look at. Yeats was dressed for the part with flowing locks and drooping tie and stately gestures, whereas Eliot appeared to want to look deliberately "unpoetic," with his neat dark hair and neat, sober city man's suit; while Siegfried Sassoon was different again: outwardly the complete fox-hunting man with his riding breeches and hacking jacket and abrupt schoolboyish mode of speech, though his beautiful brooding head and odd, impulsive movements showed him as also the imaginative poet. Garsington voices were also strikingly diverse. Opening the door, one's ear would be made aware of a murmur in which mingled the breathless staccato utterances of literary Cambridge, the emphatic drawl of literary Oxford, the vigorous Cockney of some painter bred in East London, the rich brogue of a poet bred in Dublin.

People did not bother about their accents at Garsington. Its atmosphere was so strong as to dissolve any awkwardness made by such minor differences. Major differences of personality, however, did appear; for everyone there was encouraged to be very much himself and this often meant someone distinctive and surprising. I remember Yeats on one of my first visits asking me to come and see him in Oxford, where he was living at the time. "Do not expect a party," he said. "I live very quietly, seeing only my old friends and a few witches." I never went to see him; I regret it now. But, at nineteen years old, I was daunted by the prospect of an evening alone with Yeats and some witches.

Another odd episode preserved in the picture gallery of my memories centers around the figure of Wyndham Lewis. He did not seem happy at Garsington, for his fellow guests included Virginia Woolf and other literary figures for whom he entertained paranoiac feelings as persons out to undermine civilization and in particular himself, in his view, its only true defender. Accordingly, when I arrived from Oxford, I saw him, a figure dressed in a black cloak and big black sombrero, standing solitary at the top of the grass terrace while the rest of the guests were gathered together round the pool lower down. Lady Ottoline came up and introduced me: together we paced up

and down the upper terrace. I forget our conversation, beyond the fact that I did not find it easy going; but I recall that from time to time he would stop and glance fiercely and nervously over his shoulder at the group below. Lady Ottoline watched us from a distance. When the time came for me to go, she saw me to the door. "I am not sure that I like Mr. Lewis," she said ruminatingly; and then, turning to me with an amused conspiratorial air, "Did *you* like him?" she asked.

These are comic memories, and indeed social life at Garsington and Gower Street had a comic side, it was part of its charm. All the same, my most typical memories of it are not comic but poetic or enthralling. Two such memories from the Gower Street days have especially stuck in my mind. The first was on a special occasion sometime in the early thirties. Koteliansky, a close friend of D. H. Lawrence during his lifetime, who had since gone on battling against what he believed to be the deadening orthodoxies of the past, wanted to meet T. S. Eliot. They had known each other well in earlier days but had not seen each other for years, partly because Koteliansky had been disgusted by Eliot's conversion to orthodox Anglicanism. Lately, however, he had asked Lady Ottoline if she would arrange for him to see Eliot again in order to give him a piece of his mind on the subject. She said yes: so dramatic and possibly illuminating a confrontation was just the kind of thing to appeal to her and she took care to stage it properly. Obviously it could not take place before a large audience; but she thought it deserved witnesses and accordingly invited two representatives of a younger generation, of which I was one. After tea we settled down in the drawing room; excitedly and with Slav volubility, Koteliansky launched his attack. Eliot, he said, must have turned to Christianity from a cowardly desire for comfort. Eliot rose to the occasion; his reply was deeply impressive. So far from Christianity being a comfort to him, he said, it was in some ways the reverse: for it had forced him to face the full dangers of the human predicament, not just in this life but for eternity; and it had burdened his soul with a terrible and hitherto unrealized weight of moral responsibility. What he said, however, was less important than the way he said it; briefly and restrainedly, but with such a grave sincerity of conviction that it was impossible not to believe him. Koteliansky was silenced; and I myself listening felt that I had been given a glimpse into the depths of Eliot's grand and tragic spirit. I saw that Lady Ottoline felt so too.

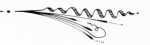

The second scene took place on an autumn evening at one of her regular gatherings. To the usual attendants was added Sara Allgood, the Irish player, a consummate artist who had created many of the principal roles in the plays of Synge and Sean O'Casey. Offstage she seemed a simple little Irishwoman who might have been expected to be shy in these exotic surroundings; for the house in Gower Street was decorated in the same style as Garsington had been. But, perhaps because she felt herself among other artists, Sara Allgood was at ease and when Lady Ottoline asked her to sing she complied at once. Still sitting in her chair at the fireside she sang, unaccompanied, some street ballads of her country. She was no longer young but her voice was still true and sweet; and she used it in such a way as to convey the sentiment of her songs with a tender pathos all the more touching from the contrast of her peasant simplicity with the dim rich beauty of the room where she sat and the hum of the great city, faintly and ceaselessly audible outside.

It seemed that Lady Ottoline's dream of the good life had for once come true, if only for a moment; that, on that autumn evening at No. 10 Gower Street, life was indeed being lived "on the same plane as poetry and as music."

THE
ALBUM

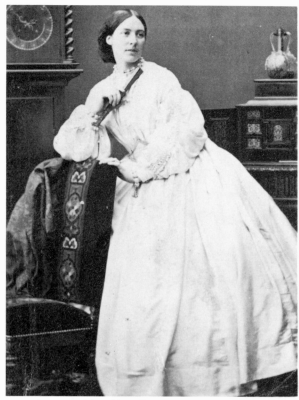

Ottoline's mother, Lady Bolsover (Mrs. Arthur Bentinck)

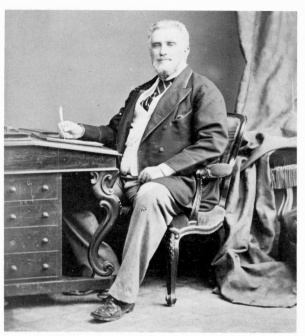

Ottoline's father, Major General Arthur Bentinck

My father died in December 1877. His cousin, the fifth Duke of Portland whom my father, if he had survived, would have succeeded, died exactly two years later. If the order of these events had been reversed and my father had lived to become Duke of Portland, as he had always expected that he would, being much the younger man, it would naturally have made a great difference to my mother and in many ways to us all. But events do not happen as mortals desire, and they must submit and accommodate themselves to them.

—*Memoirs of Lady Ottoline Morrell*

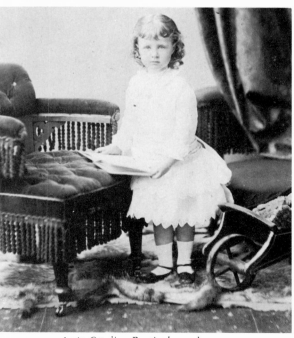

Lady Ottoline Bentinck, aged 4 or 5

She would recall her girlhood at Welbeck when she gave Bible-lessons to the servants, and commented, "It was hard to preach the gospel of Christ to fifty footmen chosen for their good looks." —C. M. BOWRA,
Memories, 1898–1939

Ottoline, aged 10, 16, and 28

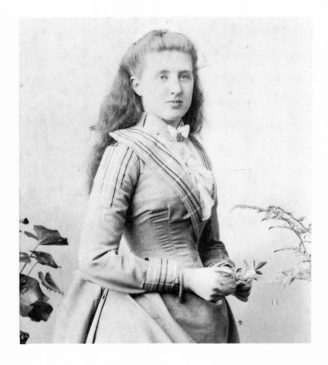

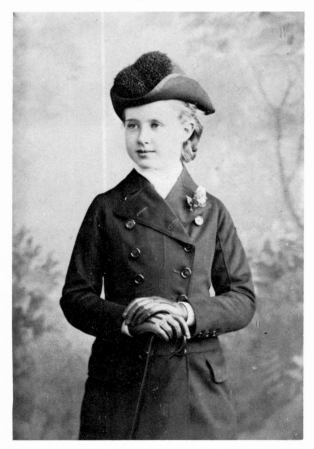

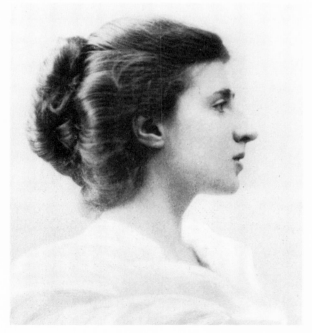

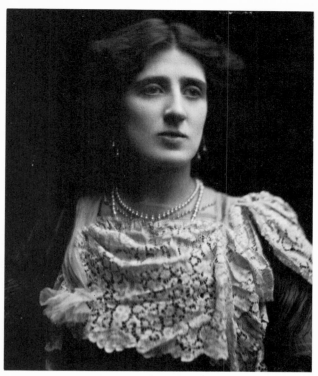

Ottoline, 1902
(photograph by H. Walter Barnett)

Once when Virginia Woolf was sitting beside Lady Ottoline on a sofa their two profiles were suddenly to be seen, one in relief against the other, like two profiles on some Renaissance medal—two strange, queenly figures evolved in the leisured and ceremonious days of the nineteenth century. Each, by being herself, won an allegiance to herself in the twentieth. Both faces were aristocratic, but in that chance propinquity Virginia Woolf's appeared much the more fine and delicate. The two women admired one another, with reservations on one side at least; and they were affectionate in manner when together, though one appeared more affectionate than the other. They had a good deal in common. Both had what old-fashioned people used to call *presence*—a kind of stateliness, a kind of simple, unfussy dignity. Lady Ottoline Morrell, not always discriminating about people, recognized the uniqueness of Virginia Woolf. Virginia Woolf spoke admiringly of the independence and force of character which had enabled Lady Ottoline to emerge from the grand but narrow world into which she had been born (and of which she retained the panache) into a more varied world in which ideas and talent counted more than property or background. —WILLIAM PLOMER, *At Home*

. . . Philip wanted to marry me. I sat up all night in my bedroom by my fire trying to push away the feeling of pressure that was closing upon me. I felt his personality almost physically elbowing in on me, a pressure of Fate. I wished to withstand it.

I didn't really think of marrying then, and clung to my solitary liberty. I believe in many women there is a strong intuitive feeling of pride in their solitary life that when marriage really comes it is, to a certain extent, a humiliation. . . .

Our wedding took place on February 8th, 1902, at St. Peter's, Eaton Square. . . .

No one could have been kinder or more generous than my family were to me then, except that my youngest brother said to Philip at the wedding, "Well, I am glad I am not in your shoes. I wouldn't undertake her for anything."

—*Memoirs of Lady Ottoline Morrell*

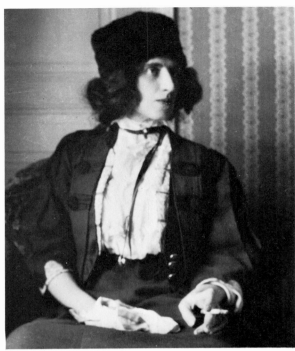

Ottoline Morrell on honeymoon, Paris, 1902

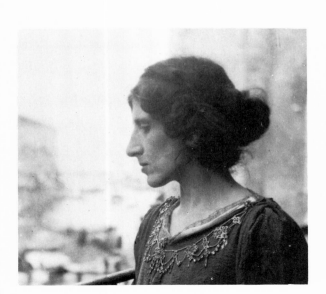

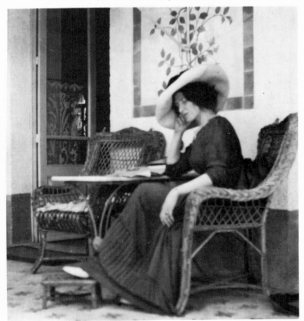

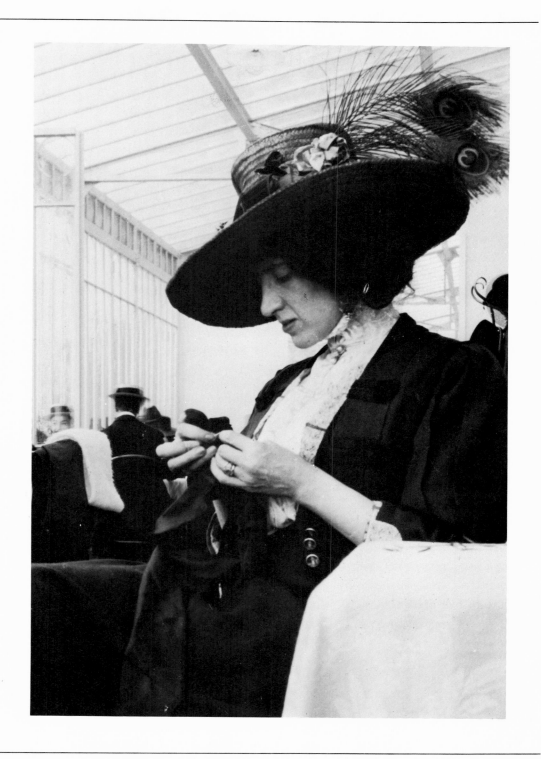

The war to [the Liberals] was not the product of German militarism but of "pre-war diplomacy," a system which they equated with the balance of power, armaments-building, and binding agreements between rival power groupings. In their view, Britain's Liberal government had gravely erred by joining in this system, and so had helped to bring about the war. As one Liberal "pacifist" M.P., Philip Morrell, put the matter in October 1916:

> I was opposed to the policy of the Triple Entente, which in my judgment was one of the principal causes leading to war, and so far from thinking that the outbreak can be attributed entirely to the exceptional wickedness of one nation or one man, I held, and still hold, that whatever may have been the special guilt of Germany, which I do not for a moment extenuate or excuse, all the governments of the Great Powers of Europe, not excluding our own, were in different degrees responsible for the outbreak.

Liberals, he said . . . should not abandon in this conflict the principles of individual liberty—free trade, free service, freedom of opinion—which had made Britain one of the best-governed and most prosperous countries in the world. And he went on:

> The system of conscription, like the system of Tariff Protection, with which it is closely allied, is in every country where it exists one of the most potent instruments of privilege and oppression. It gives to the military authorities a power over the lives of other men, and especially the lives of the workers, which is destructive of all true progress. It leads inevitably to that spirit of militarism of which the pernicious effects, as developed in Germany, are now very visible to us.

—TREVOR WILSON,
*The Downfall of the
Liberal Party, 1914–1935*

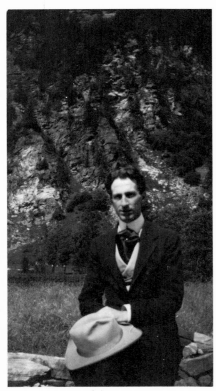

Philip, 1903

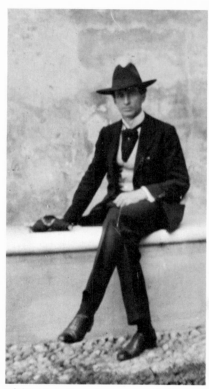

Philip Morrell on honeymoon, Paris, 1902

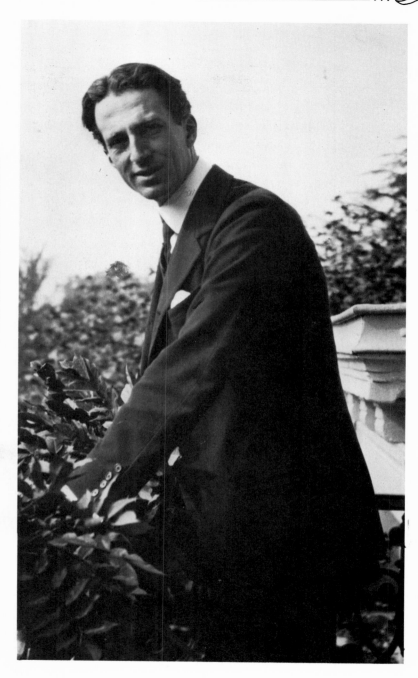

Now she came along, with her head held up, balancing an enormous flat hat of pale yellow velvet, on which were streaks of ostrich feathers, natural and grey. She drifted forward as if scarcely conscious, her long blanched face lifted up, not to see the world. She was rich. She wore a dress of silky, frail velvet, of pale yellow colour, and she carried a lot of small rose-coloured cyclamens. Her shoes and stockings were brownish grey, like the feathers on her hat, her hair was heavy, she drifted along with a peculiar fixity of the hips, a strange unwilling motion. . . . She was a woman of the new school, full of intellectuality, and heavy, nerve-worn with consciousness. She was passionately interested in reform, her soul was given up to the public cause. But she was a man's woman, it was the manly world that held her.　　　—D. H. LAWRENCE,
Women in Love

Ottoline, 1903 (photographs by Beresford)

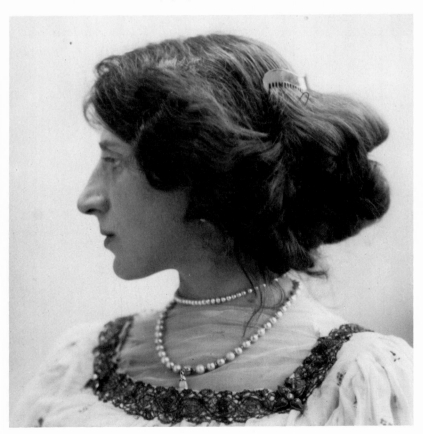

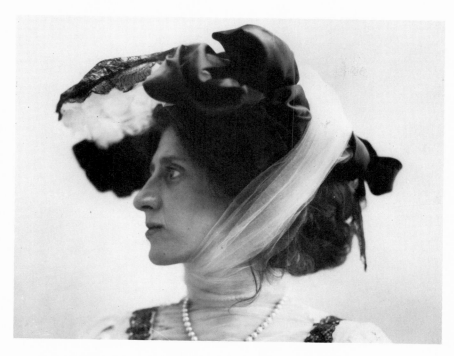

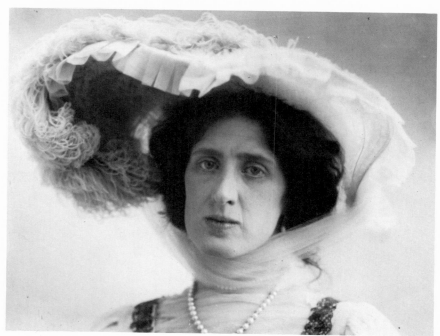

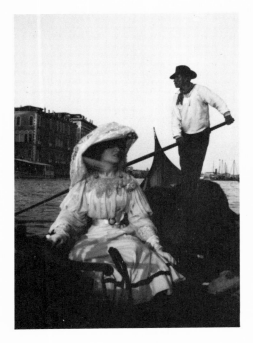 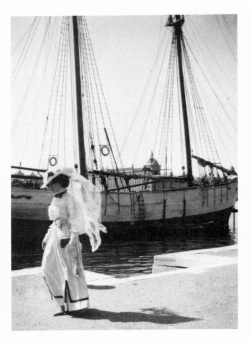

Ottoline in Venice

Italy has ever been in my imagination the land of my freedom. It is banal to say this, for I have heard it said so often by young ladies, and there has always been a pang of jealousy in the thought, for I feel sure they never felt the same joy and rapture that I felt. . . . As I look back on the years that followed, and trace my wanderings, I see I was more in Italy than in England.

—*Memoirs of Lady Ottoline Morrell*

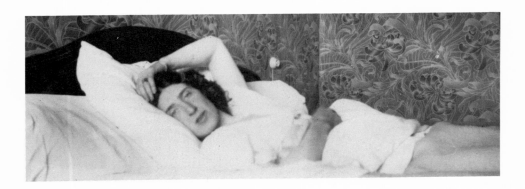

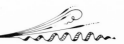

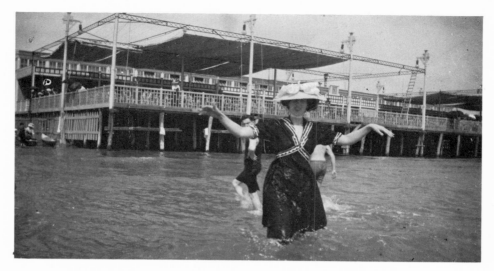

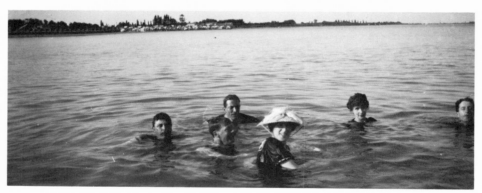

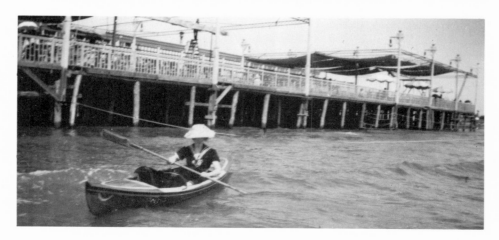

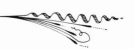

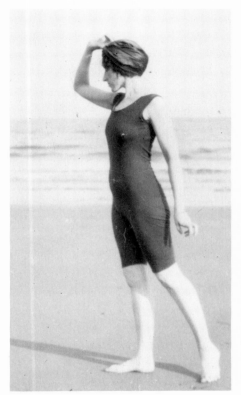

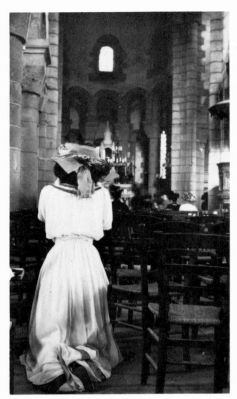

Ottoline in Venice (below, with Augustus John)

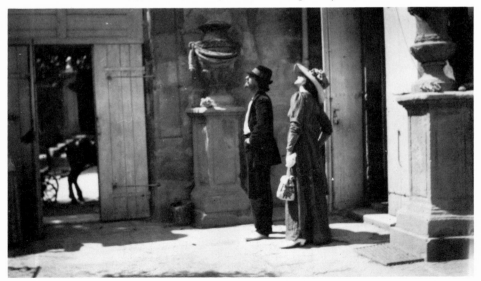

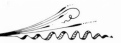

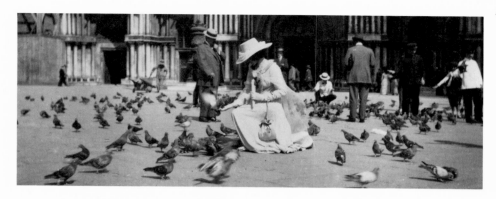

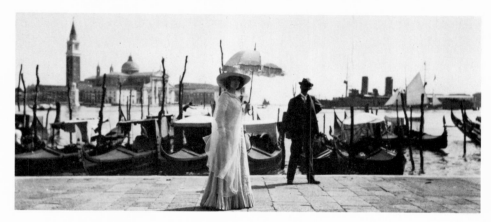

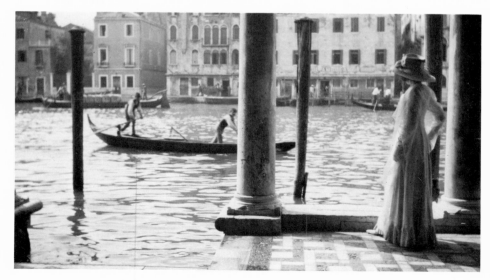

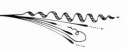

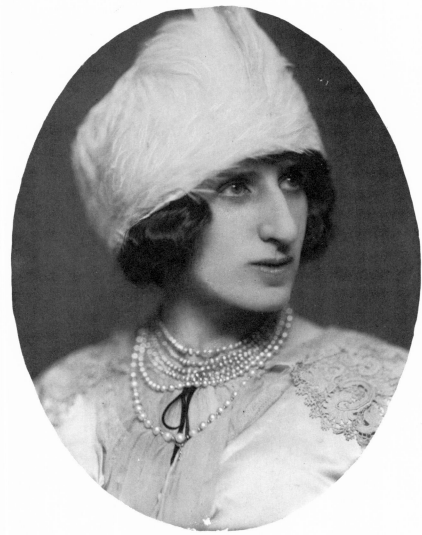

Ottoline, 1904 (photograph by Lizzie Caswall Smith)

We have just got to know a wonderful Lady Ottoline Morrell, who has the head of a Medusa; but she is very simple and innocent in spite of it, and worships the arts.

—VIRGINIA WOOLF,
as quoted in David Gadd,
The Loving Friends

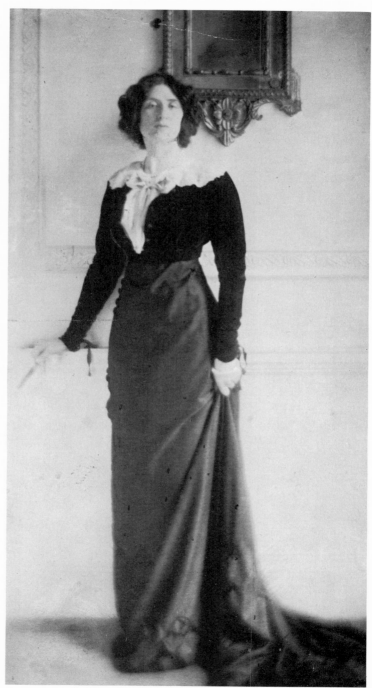

Ottoline, 1912 (photograph by Cavendish Morton)

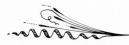

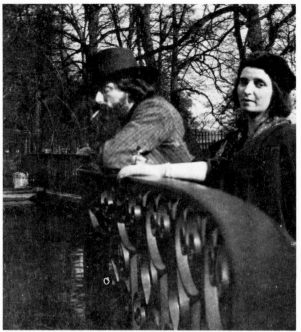

Augustus and Dorelia John at Hampton Court, 1910

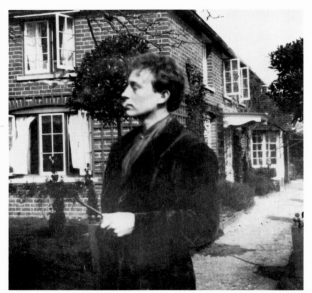

Henry Lamb at Peppard Cottage, 1911

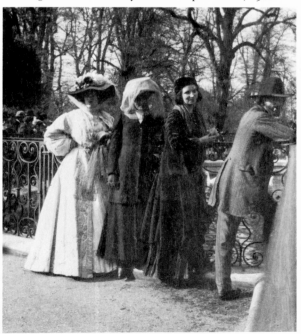

*Ottoline, possibly Miss Chadburne,
Dorelia and Augustus John*

Then there is Lady Ottoline Morrell, who fell so
violently in love with him that John recoiled from
her stream of presents and unannounced visits.
He had enjoyed the most delectable beauties of
his day, and, although he admired Lady Ottoline's
intelligence and generosity, he was clearly horri-
fied by her "prognathous jaw and bold baronial
nose," and became positively Victorian in his ef-
forts to escape. His feelings are marvellously
expressed in his portraits of her, which, to her
eternal credit, Lady Ottoline hung in her house.
Finally he got rid of her through the agency of
the ubiquitous, cold-hearted Henry Lamb who,
at that date, could be guaranteed to charm anyone of either sex.

—KENNETH CLARK,
"A Peer Gynt from the Slade,"
Times Literary Supplement

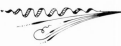

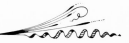

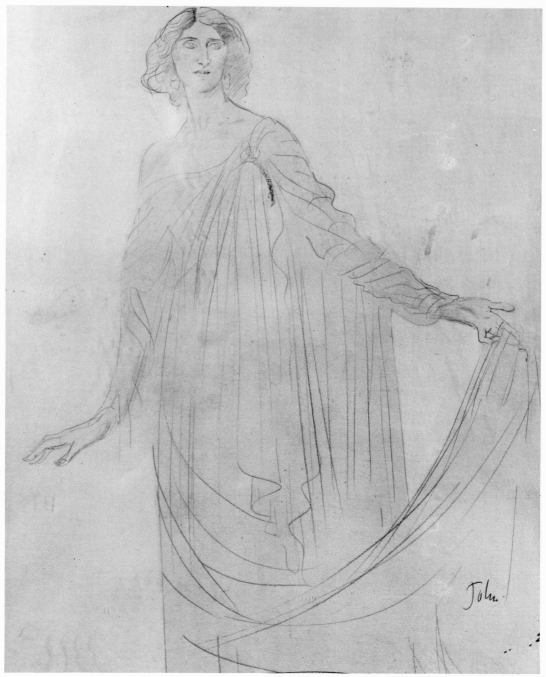

Ottoline, between 1902 and 1912 (drawing by Augustus John)

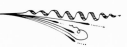

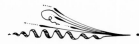

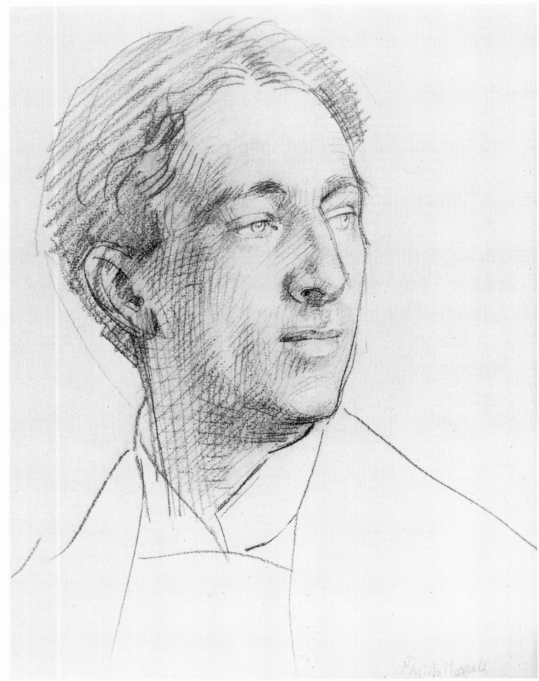

Philip Morrell, 1911 (drawing by Henry Lamb)

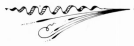

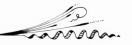

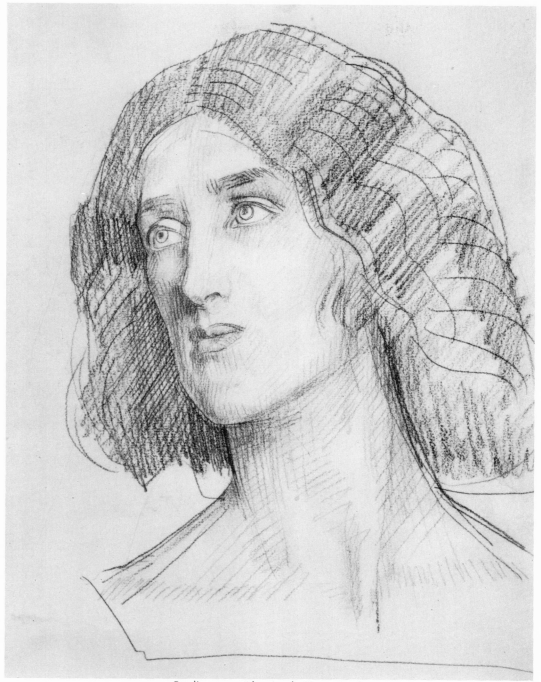

Ottoline, 1911 (drawing by Henry Lamb)

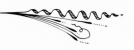

I looked forward with apprehension to the years ahead, feeling myself incapable of bringing up a child. The warm and happy maternal instinct towards an unknown child was omitted from my temperament. But when the first cry was heard, the voice of the little stranger was answered by a new and strange echo in me. That cry was not in vain—as the child awoke, so did the instinct within me.

The cry was from two lives, for I had given birth to twins at 10:30 on May 18, 1906. The little girl was so fragile and small that her life was despaired of; the little boy was apparently strong and well. But he who was our joy was taken suddenly ill on May 21st. . . . That personality that bid fair to be unique is gone. He has not tarried here, to pass through this life. . . . Where had he gone?

. . . But the little fragile sister remains, and upon her care has to be lavished to keep the flickering flame of life alight. Small hope at first, but . . . her little personality, already independent, asserts itself.

—*Memoirs of Lady Ottoline Morrell*

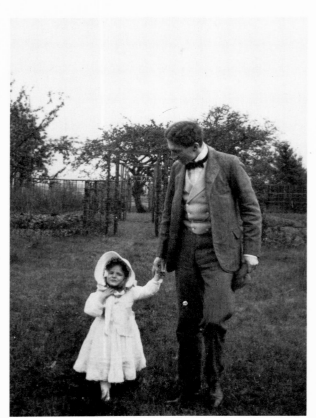

Julian and Philip Morrell at Peppard Cottage, 1910

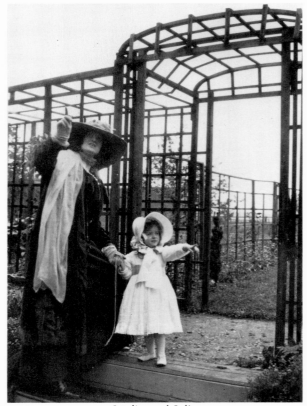

Ottoline and Julian

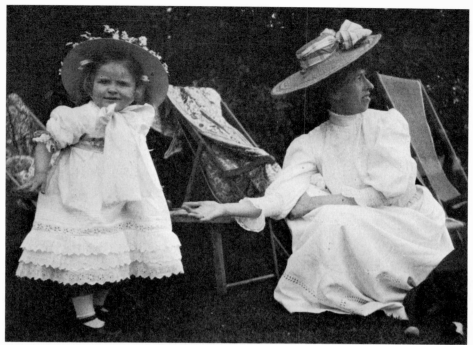

Julian Morrell and Ethel Sands, 1908

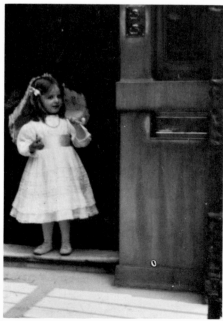

Julian at 44 Bedford Square, aged 3

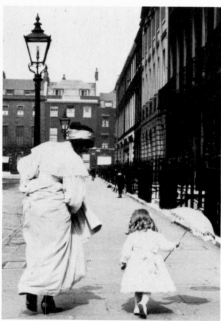

Ottoline and Julian outside 44 Bedford Square, 1908

It had not, until this moment, occurred to me that Ottoline was a woman who would allow me to make love to her, but gradually, as the evening progressed, the desire to make love to her became more and more insistent. At last it conquered, and I found to my amazement that I loved her deeply, and that she returned my feeling.

—BERTRAND RUSSELL,
Autobiography

Ottoline about 1912 (photographs by Baron de Meyer)

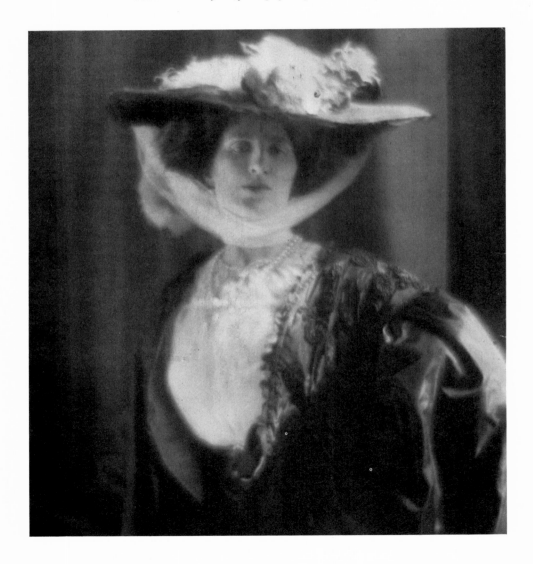

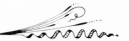

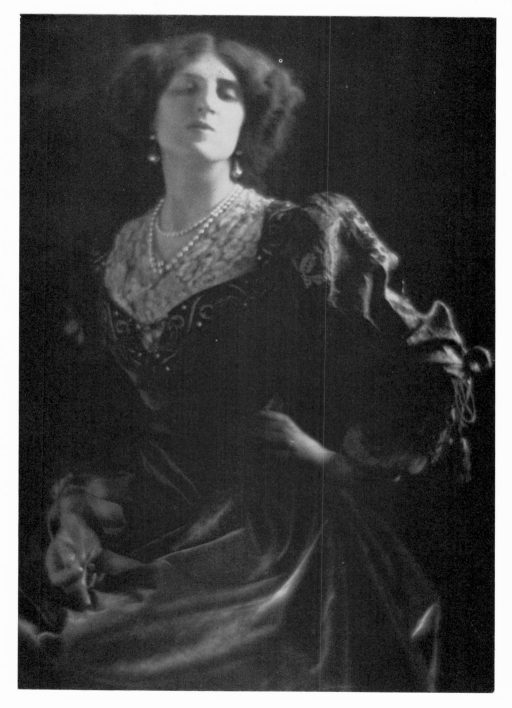

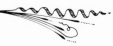

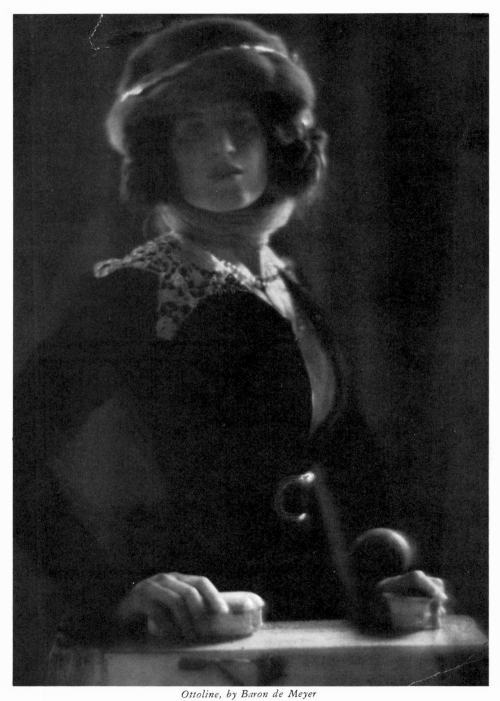

Ottoline, by Baron de Meyer

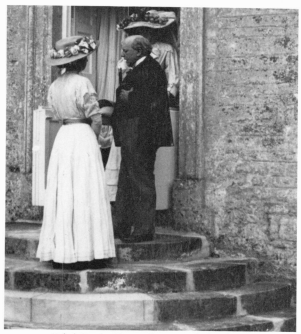

Ethel Sands, Henry James, and Ottoline

The Master took a lively interest in suffragette activities. He saw something of Lady Ottoline Morrell, "always touching and charming; and yesterday [May 8, 1912] she was very interesting; and also beautiful. But I wish she didn't run so much to the stale, but a little more to the fresh, in costume." He referred to her "window-curtaining clothes." Lady Ottoline did affect elaborate and eccentric garb; one might meet her on occasion dressed as a shepherdess.

—LEON EDEL,
Henry James: The Master, 1901–1916

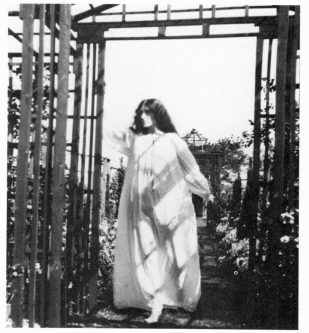

Ottoline at Peppard Cottage

. . . he warned Ottoline: "Don't be surprised if I suddenly arrive at Broughton pale and trembling —I should send a telegram first." . . . Four days later . . . he telegraphed to Ottoline:

SHALL ARRIVE TOMORROW WIRE TRAIN LATER IN NEED OF YOUR CORRAGGIO AS WELL AS MY OWN.

What then happened has been described by Ottoline herself. "He arrived soon after the telegram and fell into my arms," she recounted, "an emotional, nervous and physical wreck, ill and bruised in spirit, haunted and shocked. I comforted him and diverted him as much as I could. It was difficult to contend with the appalling weather; we gave him a sitting-room to write in, and he stayed some time. I had many an enchanting talk with him and we grew very intimate. He read aloud to me, poetry—Shakespeare, Racine and Crashaw (who carried me away by his intense passion). We took long walks together and went to see Broughton Castle where Lady Algernon Lennox was living. . . .

"At night Lytton would become gay and we would laugh and giggle and be foolish; sometimes he would put on a pair of my smart high-heeled shoes, which made him look like an Aubrey Beardsley drawing, very wicked. I love to see him in my memory tottering and pirouetting round the room with feet looking so absurdly small, peeping in and out of his trousers, both of us so excited and happy, getting more fantastic and gay."

The atmosphere at Broughton, lively, soothing, comfortable, supremely civilized, was all that Lytton could have wished for in the way of convalescence.
—MICHAEL HOLROYD,
Lytton Strachey

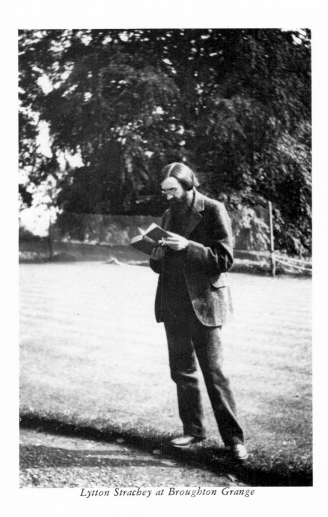
Lytton Strachey at Broughton Grange

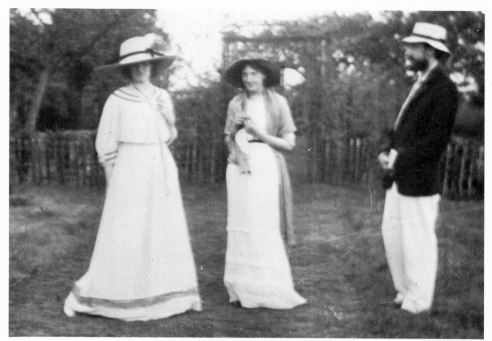

Ottoline, Vanessa Stephen, and Lytton Strachey

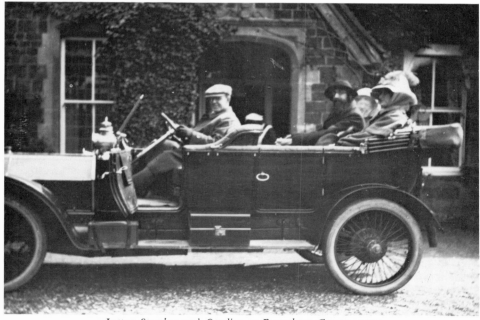

Lytton Strachey and Ottoline at Broughton Grange, 1912

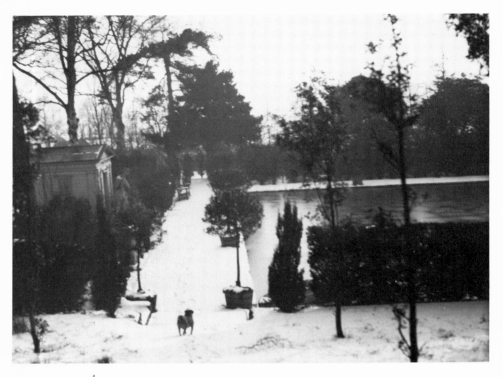

Garsington Manor, the Morrell estate near Oxford

He [Robbie Ross] did however say that the Morrells lived in an enchanting house, and I fully agreed with him when we drew up outside the tall iron gates and stood for a moment in the shadow of some lofty elms. Within the gates was a green forecourt, walled on either side by high yew hedges. Across the court a paved path led to the manor house. Viewed in the buzzing mid-afternoon stillness, the severe aloofness of the centuried grey stone front made our rattling taxi-cab seem a vulgar intrusion. Robbie remarked that he always felt an imposter when he arrived at a place like this. My only words for it were the obvious ones—"an absolute dream of beauty." It was surely no wonder that Lady Ottoline felt romantic and poetical in such surroundings! Having discreetly jangled the bell we were greeted by distant barkings, and when the ancient oak door was opened an officious little pug bustled out to give us a noisy greeting.

—SIEGFRIED SASSOON,
Siegfried's Journey

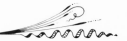

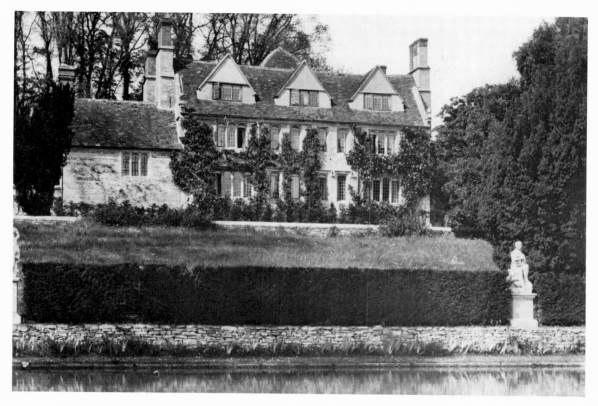

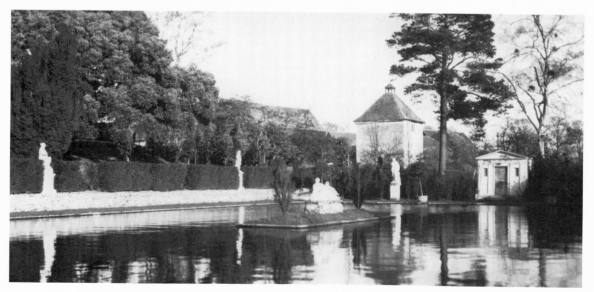

O what if gardens where the peacock strays
With delicate feet upon old terraces,
Or else all Juno from an urn displays
Before the indifferent garden deities;
O what if levelled lawns and gravelled ways
Where slippered Contemplation finds his ease
And Childhood a delight for every sense,
But take our greatness with our violence?

        —W. B. YEATS,

              "Meditations in Time of Civil War"

Garsington Manor

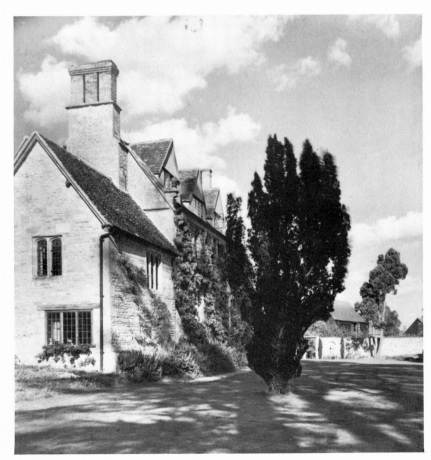

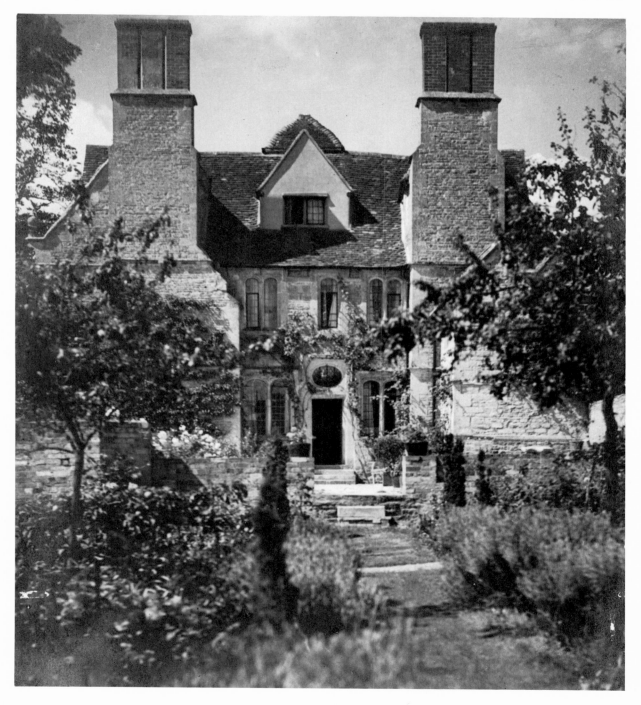

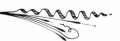

Inside there were several large panelled rooms, which had, I surmise, been a mixture of genuine seventeenth century and Victorian baronial styles before Ottoline descended upon them. She had transformed them, stamping her personality ruthlessly everywhere. The oak panelling had been painted a dark peacock blue-green; the bare and sombre dignity of Elizabethan wood and stone had been overwhelmed with an almost oriental magnificence: the luxuries of silk curtains and Persian carpets, cushions and pouffes. Ottoline's pack of pug dogs trotted everywhere and added to the Beardsley quality, which was one half of her natural taste. The characteristic of every house in which Ottoline lived was its smell and the smell of Garsington was stronger than that of Bedford Square. It reeked of the bowls of pot-pourri and orris-root which stood on every mantelpiece, side table and window-sill and of the desiccated oranges, studded with cloves, which Ottoline loved making. The walls were covered with a variety of pictures. Italian pictures and bric-à-brac, drawings by John, water-colours for fans by Conder, who was rumoured to have been one of Ottoline's first conquests, paintings by Duncan and Gertler and a dozen other of the younger artists.   —DAVID GARNETT,

The Flowers of the Forest

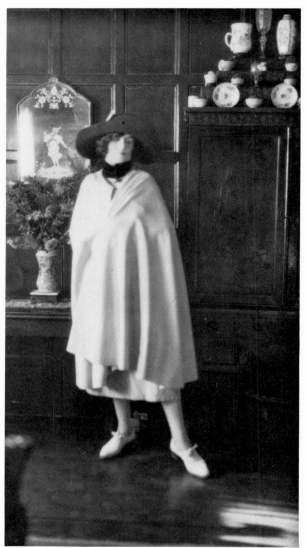

Ottoline in the Red Room at Garsington

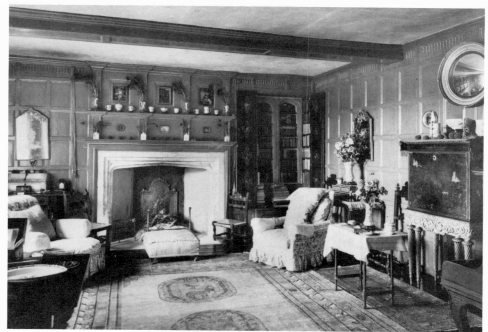

The Red Room

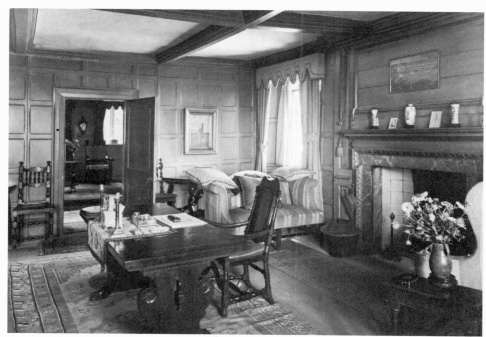

The Green Room

While other guests came and went, [Mark Gertler] and Brett, who had become a close friend of Ottoline's, were the "painters in residence."

"I love working all day here and then the pleasant meal in the evening, with either the pianola or reading afterwards," Mark declared. They would lounge in "incredibly comfortable" armchairs in front of the enormous log fire. . .

In the day time, if Mark's work went wrong, he could seize upon someone to walk with at any moment or join in a game of croquet.

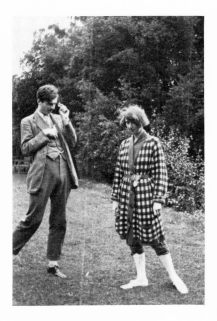

Brett was a great comfort. "She is invaluable, she is so good. She understands me and my work and what I want to do better than anyone—I do love her for this," he announced. "How much she helps me, even to domestic details—such as washing my hair. Once she even came on her own account to scrub my back in the bath! This place has spoilt me! How shall I live without all this now! Brett has real talent too" (12 September 1917). Brett had supported all his experiments, being "frightfully excited" about his sculpture and "very pleased" that he was writing.

—JOHN WOODESON,
Mark Gertler

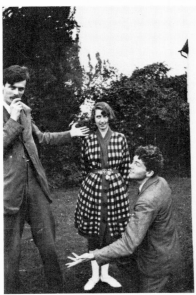

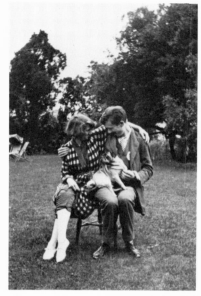
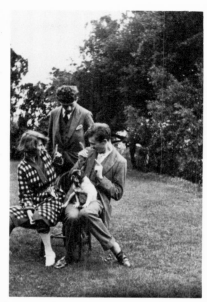
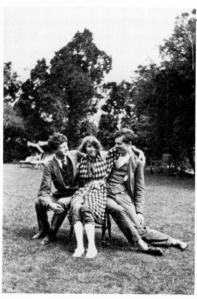

Mark Gertler, Dorothy Brett, and a mustachioed Aldous Huxley

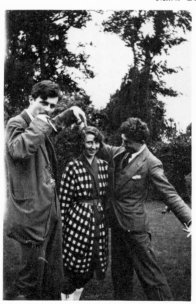
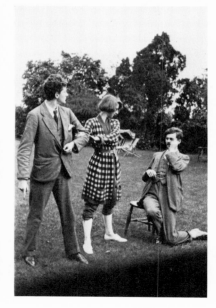
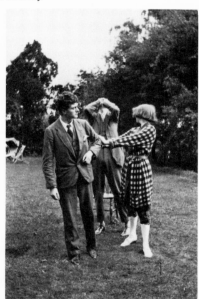

Garsington was anti-war. Philip Morrell, Liberal M.P. for Burnley, was one of the few men in public life who spoke up against it. He and Lady Ottoline made Garsington a refuge for some extremely civilized conscientious objectors. On the home farm—run by Philip with loving care—men like Bertrand Russell, Clive Bell and Gerald Shove, the Cambridge scholars, were able to do the agricultural work they had been sentenced to by the tribunals without too great a break in their mental and physical habits.

So there was . . . Clive Bell, "kind-hearted with a noisy voice whom the farmers loved though he never did a lick of work, giving birthday cakes to the farmers' wives."

—SYBILLE BEDFORD,
Aldous Huxley

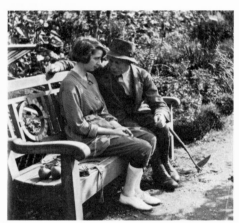

Dorothy Brett and Clive Bell

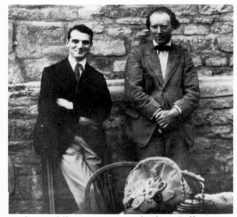

John Middleton Murry and Clive Bell, 1917

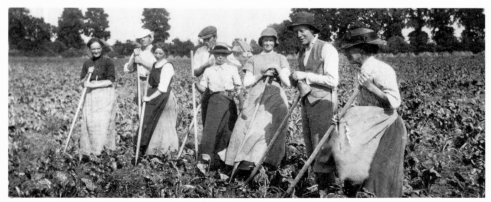

Clive Bell (second from right) with farm workers at Garsington, 1917

My dear Katherine:

. . . Do not be sad. It is one life which is passing away from us, one "I" is dying; but there is another coming into being, which is the happy, creative you. I knew you would have to die with your brother; you also, go down into a death and be extinguished. But for us there is a rising from the grave, there is a resurrection, and a clean life to begin from the start, new and happy. Don't be afraid, don't doubt it, it is so.

You have gone further into your death than Murry has. He runs away. But one day he too will submit, he will dare to go down, and be killed, to die in this self which he is. Then he will become a man; not till. He is not a man yet.

—D. H. LAWRENCE,
Collected Letters

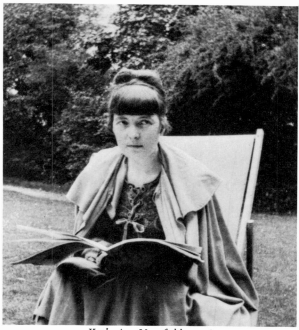

Katherine Mansfield, 1916

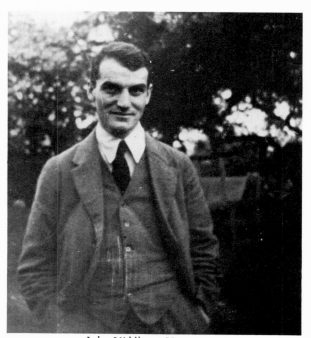

John Middleton Murry, 1916

The stranger approached. He was a young man in his early twenties, hook-nosed with blue eyes and silky pale hair that blew about in the wind—for he wore no hat. He had on a Norfolk jacket, ill cut and of cheap material, and a pair of baggy grey-flannel trousers. His tie was red. . . .

"I'm trespassing here," said the stranger. "Do you mind?" The seriousness of his defiance deepened. He looked at them sombrely. The young men were examining him from the other side of the bars, from a long way off, from the vantage ground of another class. They had noticed his clothes. There was hostility and contempt in their eyes. There was also a kind of fear. "I'm a trespasser," he repeated. —ALDOUS HUXLEY,
Point Counter Point

I saw a very great deal of Lawrence—for me, at least, the dove brooded over him, too. I loved him. He was just his old, merry, rich self, laughing, describing things, giving you pictures, full of enthusiasm and joy in a future where we become all "vagabonds" —we simply did not talk about people. We kept to things like nuts and cowslips and fires in woods and his black self *was* not. Oh, there is something so loveable about him and his eagerness, his passionate eagerness for life—that is what one loves so. Now he is gone back to the country. —KATHERINE MANSFIELD,
Letters

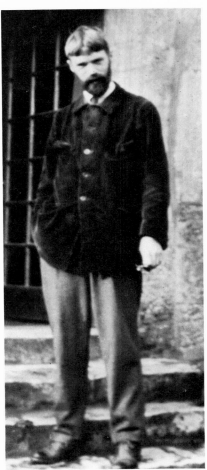

D. H. Lawrence, 1915

Our friends were going off to the war with their noble young heads in the air, to be thrown to death by incompetent strategists. He was long and dreadfully vulnerable-looking, with very soft hair, and he draped himself over things, his long arms and legs dangling across the backs of chairs or sofas. I at sixteen had got engaged to be married to a young officer—Dick Mitchison, to whom I have been married for nearly fifty years. My brother was in the Black Watch waiting for orders to go out to Flanders. Aldous and I were together a good deal and he stood by me in my fears and anxieties and above all helped to give me a more adult outlook. . . .

. . . I was never allowed to go to Garsington, though I longed to. It sounded like a world of the more than grown-up. My mother so much disliked the idea of anyone enjoying themselves during "the Great War" that she couldn't bring herself to let me go. . . . Aldous thought this very silly. . . . I was much teased by my family. Aldous never teased me and never treated me as a child. Instead he asked me difficult questions like "are you in love?" And then "describe it to me." And I twiddled my engagement ring and could only answer in terms of poems I had read and what I supposed a girl should be feeling. And all the time I was admiring the yellow tie and white socks that Aldous had already begun wearing. And I did sometimes wish he would kiss me, but I didn't know how to get him to.

—NAOMI MITCHISON,
Huxley Memorial Volume

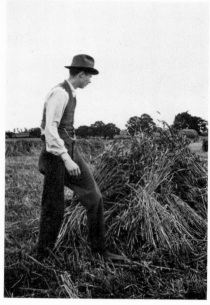

Aldous Huxley at Garsington, 1915

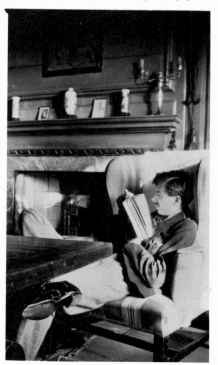

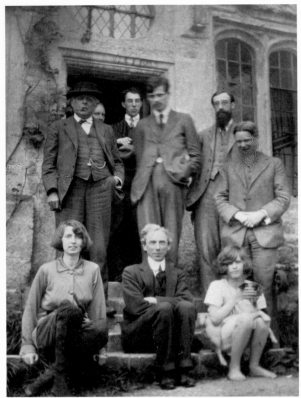

TOP: *Augustine Birrell, Philip Morrell, Francis Birrell, Aldous Huxley, Lytton Strachey, H. R. L. Sheppard.*
BOTTOM: *Dorothy Brett, Bertrand Russell, Julian Morrell*

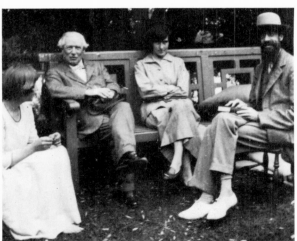

Dora Carrington, H. H. Asquith, Alix Sargant-Florence, and Lytton Strachey, 1917 or 1918

Tuesday
July 2, 1918

To Mrs. Virginia Woolf

I love to hear of Lytton's success. It seems quite measureless to man. I put my head out of window at night and expect to find his name pricked upon the heavens in real stars. I feel he is become already a sort of myth, a kind of legend. Modern princelings are hushed to sleep with tales of him and grave young duchesses disguise themselves at their Fairs and Pageants with . . . the delicate beard, the moonlight hat, the shy, reluctant umbrella. . . .

—KATHERINE MANSFIELD,
Letters

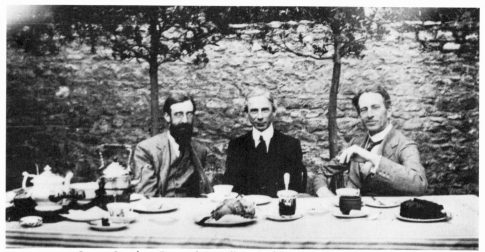

Lytton Strachey, Bertrand Russell, and Philip Morrell, 1917 or 1918

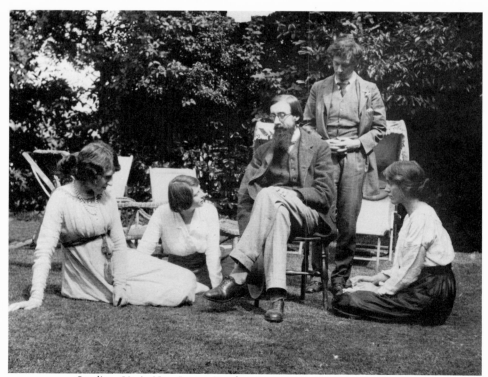

Ottoline, Maria Nys, Lytton Strachey, Duncan Grant, and Vanessa Bell

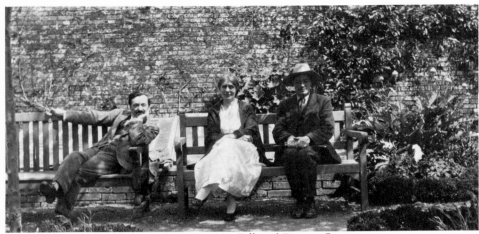

Simon Bussy, Vanessa Bell, and Duncan Grant

Maynard was the object of attack because he was in a particularly difficult position. He had risen with rapidity to a post of great responsibility and importance, and he was aware of hundreds of secrets which he could not divulge in order to justify his opinions, when they were challenged by his friends. Impatience and irritability were the natural consequences. It is perhaps significant that Duncan, who knew Maynard better than anyone, never added a word to the chorus of criticism. I think he alone understood and made full allowance for the difficulty of Maynard's position.

... I think their critical attitude at this time was a factor of great importance in Maynard's career. One of the chief characteristics of his great intelligence was the capacity to see both sides of a question, and the criticisms and anxieties of his friends led him to a stricter examination of his own motives and of the policies which he had to advocate as a servant of the Government, than he would otherwise have made. It was because his friends kept him aware of the danger that he might, for the sake of a brilliant official career, be a party to bringing about terrible evils, that he finally took the course he did in resigning his post rather than accept the reparations clauses of the Peace Treaty. That resignation led to the writing of *The Economic Consequences of the Peace* which was the foundation of his subsequent fame. —DAVID GARNETT,

The Flowers of the Forest

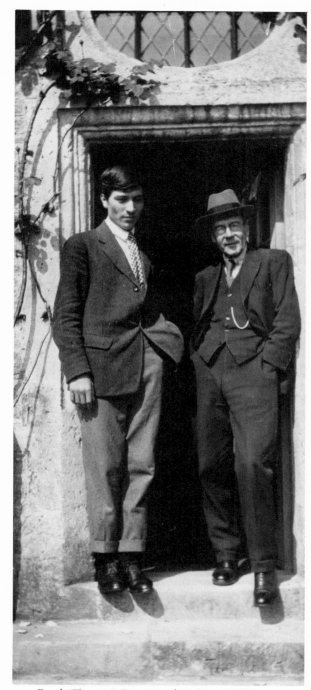

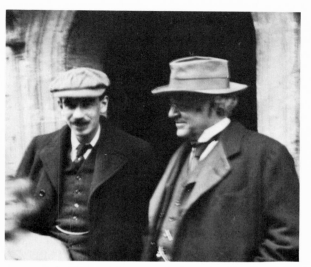

John Maynard Keynes and Augustine Birrell
at Garsington, 1917

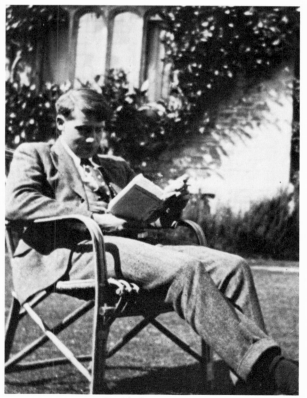

Frank "Toronto" Prewett and G. Lowes Dickinson

David Garnett, 1915

. . . I felt if I was ever to have children I could not put it off any longer. Dora was entirely willing to have children, with or without marriage, and from the first we used no precautions. She was a little disappointed to find that almost immediately our relations took on all the character of marriage, and when I told her that I should be glad to get a divorce and marry her, she burst into tears, feeling, I think, that it meant the end of independence and lightheartedness. But the feeling we had for each other seemed to have that kind of stability that made any less serious relation impossible. Those who have known her only in her public capacity would scarcely credit the quality of elfin charm which she possessed whenever the sense of responsibility did not weigh her down. Bathing by moonlight, or running with bare feet on the dewy grass, she won my imagination as completely as on her serious side she appealed to my desire for parenthood and my sense of social responsibility.
—BERTRAND RUSSELL,
Autobiography

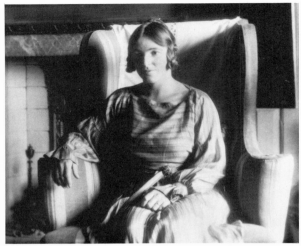

Dora Russell

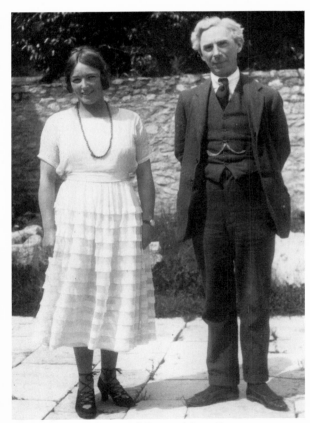

Dora and Bertrand Russell

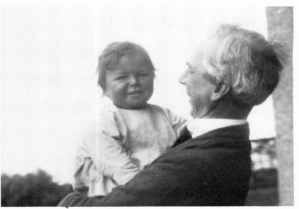

*John Conrad Russell,
with his father, Lord Russell*

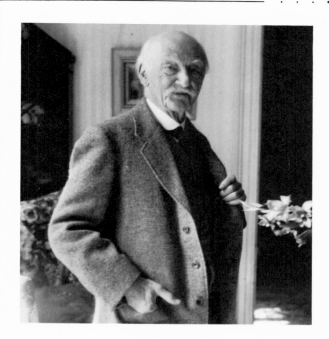

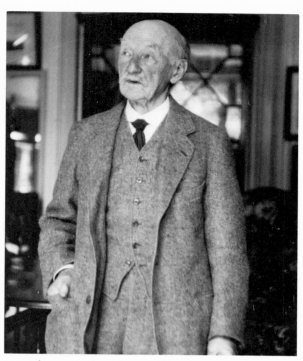

Thomas Hardy at home at Max Gate, around 1922

What I valued most in Hardy, then, as I still do, was his hawk's vision, his way of looking at life from a very great height, as in the stage directions of *The Dynasts*, or the opening chapter of *The Return of the Native*. To see the individual life related not only to the local social life of its time, but to the whole of human history, life on the earth, the stars, gives one both humility and self-confidence. For from such a perspective the difference between the individual and society is so slight, since both are so insignificant, that the latter ceases to appear as a formidable god with absolute rights, but rather as an equal, subject to the same laws of growth and decay, and therefore one with whom reconciliation is possible.

—W. H. AUDEN,
"A Literary Transference"

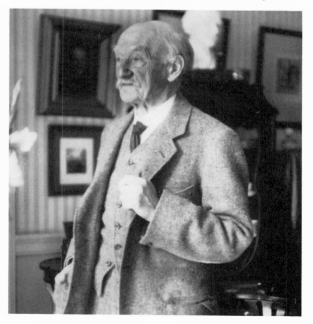

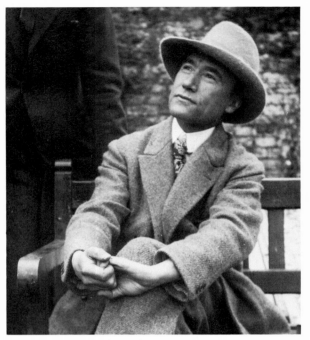

André Gide at Garsington

. . . Distinguished as ever, [Gide] was also content. I realised more clearly how much he had got out of life, and had managed to transmit through his writings. Not life's greatness—greatness is a nineteenth-century perquisite, a Goethean jog. But life's complexity, and the delight, the difficulty, the duty of registering that complexity and of conveying it. Unlike some others who have apprehended complexity, he was a hard worker. He wrote and wrote and travelled and wrote, and oh how he has helped us in consequence! He has taught thousands of people to mistrust façades, to call the bluff, to be brave without bounce and inconsistent without frivolity. He is the humanist of our age—not of other ages, but of this one.

—E. M. FORSTER,
Two Cheers for Democracy

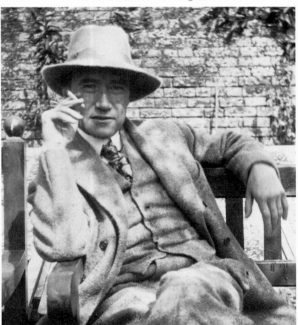

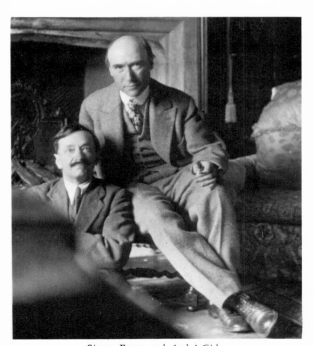

Simon Bussy and André Gide

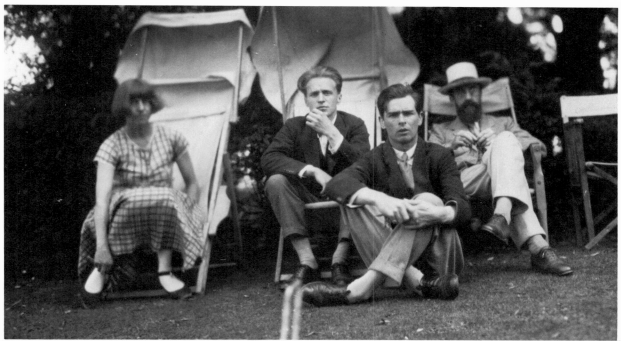

Dora Carrington, Stephen Tomlin, Sebastian Sprott, and Lytton Strachey

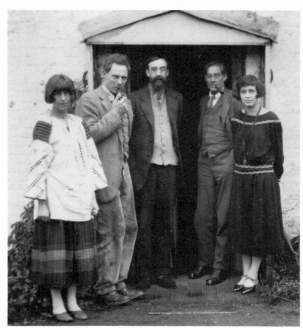

*Dora Carrington, Ralph Partridge, Lytton Strachey,
Oliver Strachey, and Ray Garnett*

Since you are bored with praise of your creations, I will tell you that I think you are the most eminent, graceful person. The most worthy, learned and withal charming character. And I shall always love you in your entirety. You know Dear Lytton it has been rather amazing living with you For so long. Now that I am alone and think or ponder on or over it. Visions steal up—of those hot days when you wore your Fakire clothes—in the orchard—The one afternoon when I saw you in the baTH.—When I lay on your bed on Thursday And smelT your hair, and broke the crackling beard in my fingers. —DORA CARRINGTON
to Lytton Strachey

... For the moment [Forster] lies out of reach and won't give up his secret. And he had a secret —it's not just sentimental to say it: nothing so spectacular as "voices," but he knew how to live in daily touch with his own depths. This set him apart, so that it was no mistake for people to have reverenced him—as they did and do. He was a rare creature, contrived of the strangest materials. —P. N. FURBANK,

"The Personality of E. M. Forster," *Encounter*

Another visit I paid him, again when he was out of sorts, to his Chiswick flat, has stayed in my memory and is relevant. It was some fifteen years ago. I had an Alsatian bitch at that time and, when he invited me over, asked if I might bring her. Starting early, I could walk much of the way from Putney and thus combine my visit with her exercise. Morgan did not like dogs (a bad mark!), he was, if anything in the animal line, a cat man, but he agreed and we reached him by noon. He was in bed and I sat beside him on the edge of it. There was something particular he wanted to tell me, naturally I forget what, and while he was speaking my dog barked. She had heard a latchkey turn in the flat's front door. It was Morgan's char arriving. I hushed her, but it was difficult to silence her in such matters in which she thought she knew best—and it was of course correct behaviour for her to bark. Morgan resumed his interrupted story, she barked again, for the char could now be heard moving about in the kitchen alongside us. With a gesture of fatigue and despair Morgan stopped once more, then resumed when I pulled the animal between my legs and tried to deprive her of further speech by gripping her jaws together with my hands. But she freed herself from this uncomfortable clamp and barked again. "Bloody dog!" exclaimed Morgan. Much embarrassed I said, "I'm so sorry" and cuffed the good creature who was only trying to warn us that there was a stranger in the place, and the stranger that he or she had been detected. Then I glanced at Morgan who had become silent. Tears were trickling down his face. He said, "Joe, forgive me. It was so *rude*." To some people this may not look a very saintly story, to me it seemed divinely beautiful that anyone should cry for such a reason. It may be added that later on, when I had published a book about this dog, he said, "Thank you, you have opened my eyes," and then chose it for one of the Sunday papers as the best book of the year.

—J. R. ACKERLEY,
E. M. Forster: A Portrait

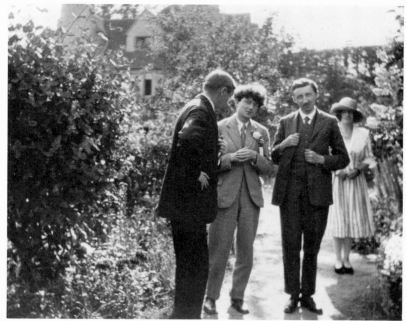

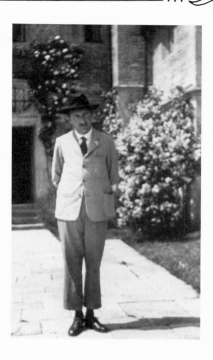

Mark Gertler, E. M. Forster, and Julian Morrell, 1926.
Man at left is unidentified.

E. M. Forster at Garsington, 1922

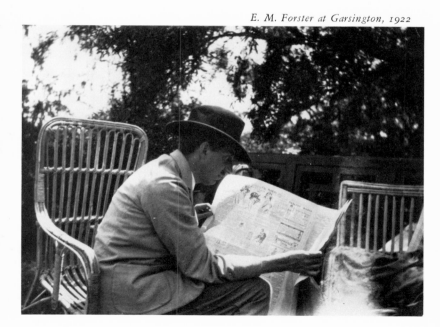

I turn away and shut the door, and on the stair
Wonder how many times I could have proved my worth
In something that all others understand or share;
But O! ambitious heart, had such a proof drawn forth
A company of friends, a conscience set at ease,
It had but made us pine the more. The abstract joy,
The half-read wisdom of daemonic images,
Suffice the ageing man as once the growing boy.

—W. B. YEATS,
"Meditations in Time of Civil War"

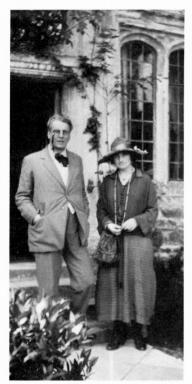

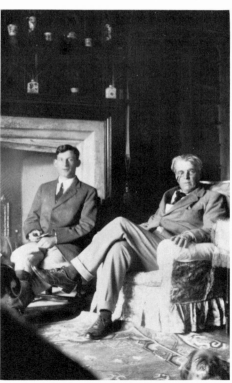

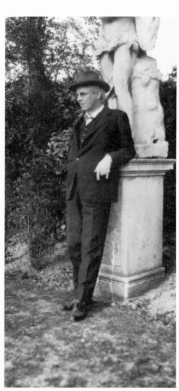

W. B. Yeats,
and his wife, George, 1922

Siegfried Sassoon and W. B. Yeats

W. B. Yeats

Mark remembered little of the voyage. "From what I used to hear of it from my brothers and sisters it was, for the most part, like a nightmare," he wrote. "We travelled in some sort of cattle boat herded very close together, the journey lasting for weeks, and most of the time in rough seas, when they were all sick and in a dreadful plight . . . it is quite at the end of the journey, our landing, in fact, when my memory comes to life . . . I am standing on a wooden floor; there is land, England; England is moving towards me—not I to it. It is sort of *gyrating* towards me. I am standing by my family all ready with heavy packages straining from their necks—pressing their backs—all available limbs are grasping rebellious packages. My mother strains her eyes and says, 'Oh, woe is me, but I cannot see your father! He is not there, he is not there, what shall I do?' "

—JOHN WOODESON,
Mark Gertler

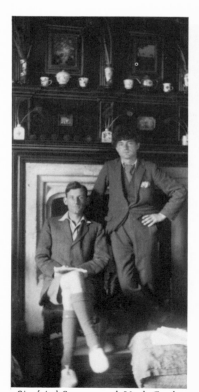

Siegfried Sassoon and Mark Gertler

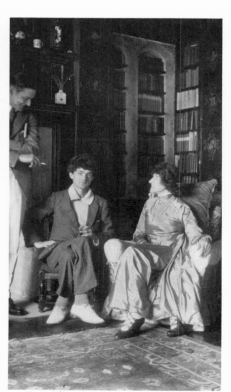

T. S. Eliot, Mark Gertler, and Ottoline

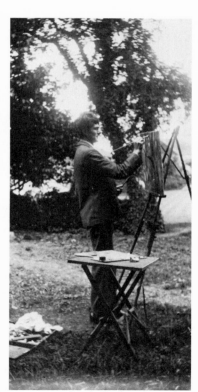

Mark Gertler

In October 1919, I went to Oxford at last . . . getting permission from St. John's College to live five miles out, on Boar's Hill—where John Masefield, who thought well of my poetry, had offered to rent us a cottage at the bottom of his garden. . . .

The Anglo-Saxon lecturer was candid about his subject: it was, he said, a language of purely linguistic interest, and hardly a line of Anglo-Saxon poetry extant possessed the slightest literary merit. I disagreed. I thought of Beowulf lying wrapped in a blanket among his platoon of drunken thanes in the Gothland billet. . . . Edmund Blunden, who also had leave to live on Boar's Hill because of gassed lungs, was taking the same course. The War still continued for both of us and we translated everything into trench-warfare terms. . . .

A number of poets were living on Boar's Hill; too many, Edmund and I agreed. It was now almost a tourist centre.   —ROBERT GRAVES,
Good-bye to All That

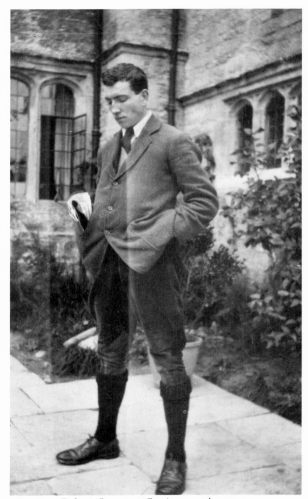

Robert Graves at Garsington, about 1920

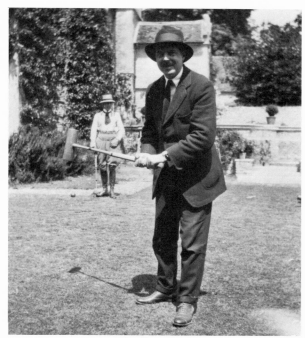

Wyndham Lewis

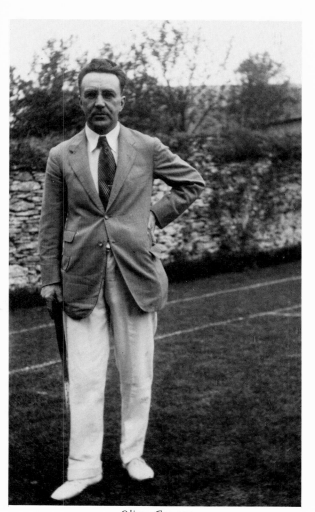

Oliver Gogarty

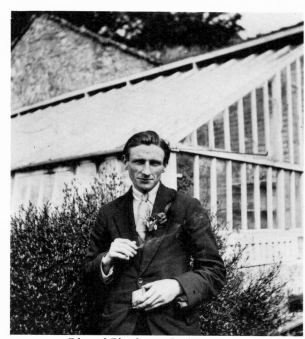

Edmund Blunden at Garsington, 1922

So here I am, in the middle way, having had twenty years—
Twenty years largely wasted, the years of l'entre deux guerres—
Trying to learn to use words, and every attempt
Is a wholly new start, and a different kind of failure
Because one has only learnt to get the better of words
For the thing one no longer has to say, or the way in which
One is no longer disposed to say it.   —T. S. ELIOT,
                                                          "East Coker"

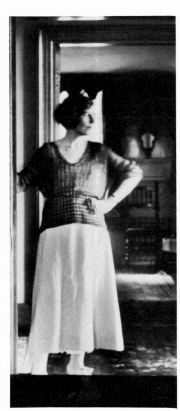
Vivienne Eliot, T. S. Eliot's first wife

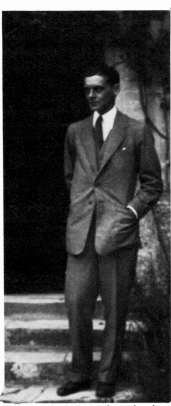
Henry Eliot, T. S. Eliot's brother

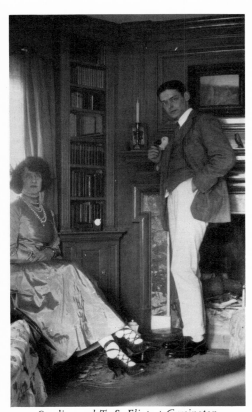
Ottoline and T. S. Eliot at Garsington

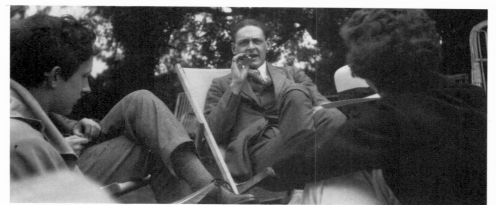

T. S. Eliot with visiting undergraduates (including Lord David Cecil, left) at Garsington

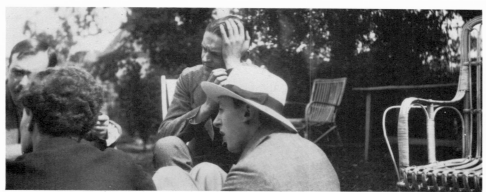

L. P. Hartley, Anthony "Puffin" Asquith, T. S. Eliot, and Eddy Sackville-West

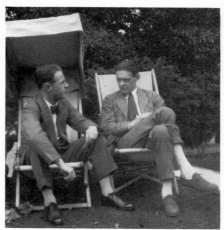

L. A. G. Strong and T. S. Eliot

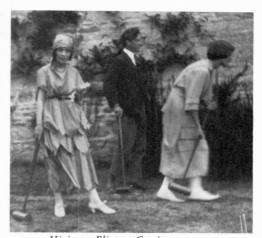

Vivienne Eliot at Garsington, 1922

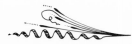

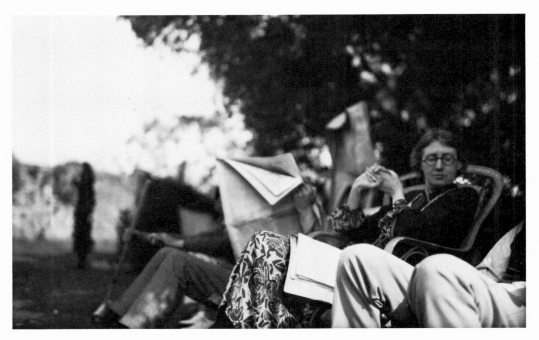

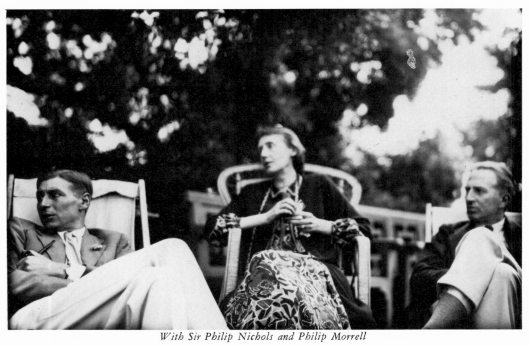

With Sir Philip Nichols and Philip Morrell

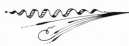

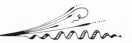

. . . She liked good talk, good food (and plenty of salt with it) and good coffee. I see her in a shady hat and summer sleeves, moving between the fig trees and the zinnias; I see her sitting over a fire and smoking one of her favorite cheroots; I see the nervous shoulders, the creative wrists, the unprecedented sculpture of the temples and eye-sockets; I see her grave and stately, or in a paroxysm of happy laughter. . . .

—WILLIAM PLOMER,
Recollections of Virginia Woolf

Virginia Woolf at Garsington

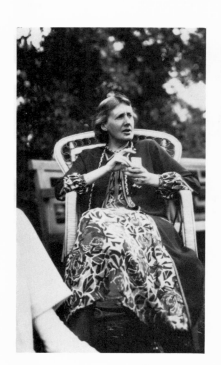 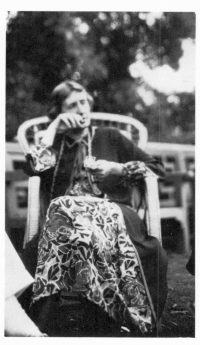 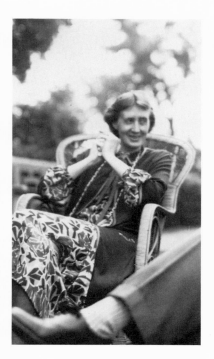

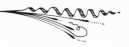

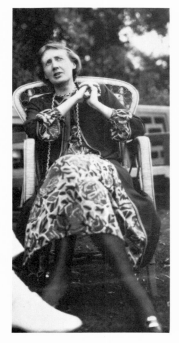
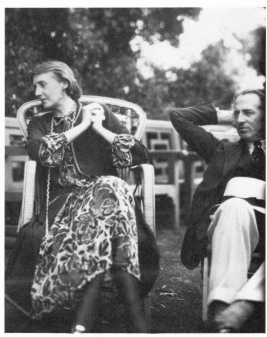
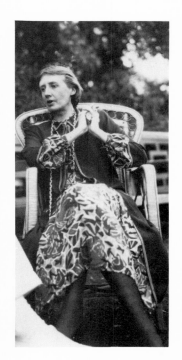

With Philip Morrell (above)

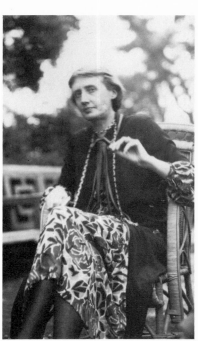
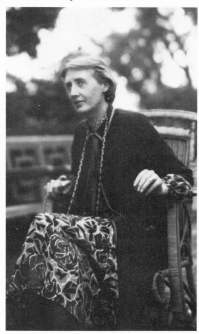
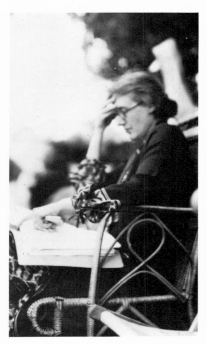

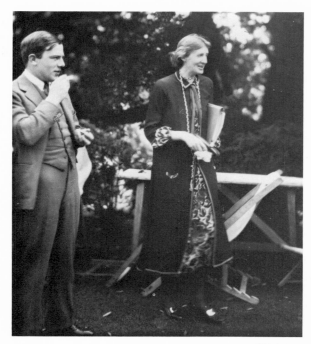

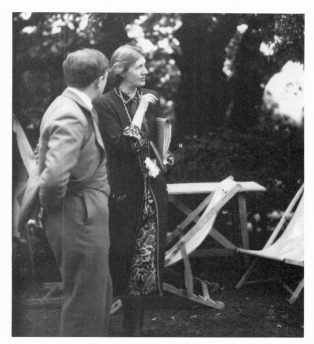

With Sir Maurice Bowra

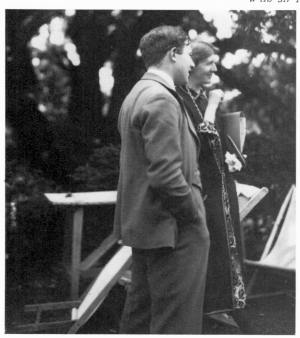

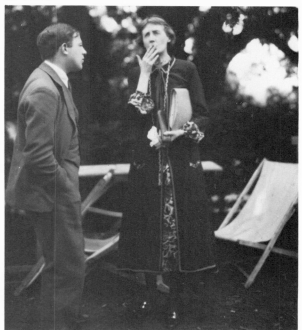

. . . With what imperious directness, like that of an artist intolerant of the conventional and the humdrum, [Ottoline] singled out the people she admired for qualities that she was often the first to detect and champion, and brought them together at Bedford Square and then at Garsington. . . . Whether she sat at her table against a background of pale yellow and pomegranate, or mused at Garsington with her embroidery on her lap and undergraduates at her feet . . . she created her own world. And it was a world in which conflicts and collisions were inevitable; nor did she escape the ridicule of those whom she befriended.

—VIRGINIA WOOLF,

in her obituary of Ottoline Morrell

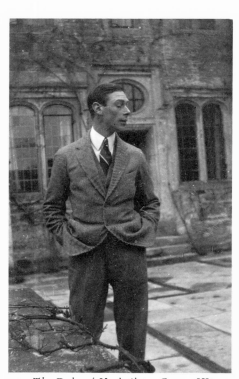

The Duke of York (later George VI)

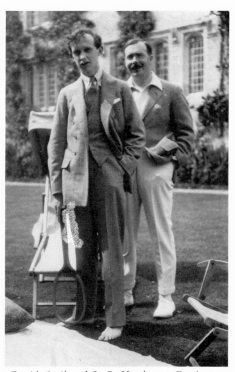

David Cecil and L. P. Hartley at Garsington

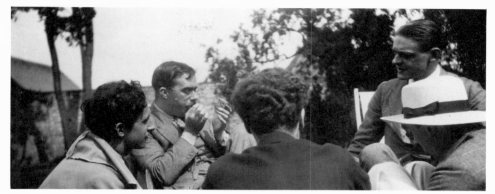

David Cecil, L. P. Hartley, Anthony Asquith, T. S. Eliot, and Eddy Sackville-West

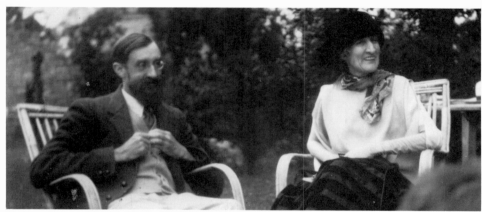

Lytton Strachey and Margot Asquith

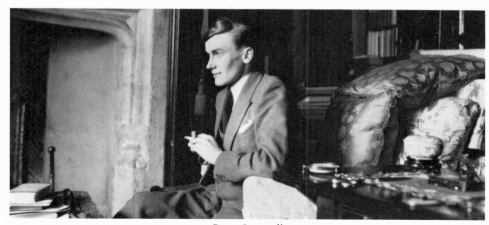

Peter Quennell

. . . I remember spending some dark, uneasy, winter days during the first war in the depth of the country with Lytton Strachey. After lunch, as we watched the rain pour down and premature darkness roll up, he said, in his searching, personal way, "Loves apart, whom would you most like to see coming up the drive?" I hesitated a moment and he supplied the answer: "Virginia of course."

—CLIVE BELL,
Old Friends

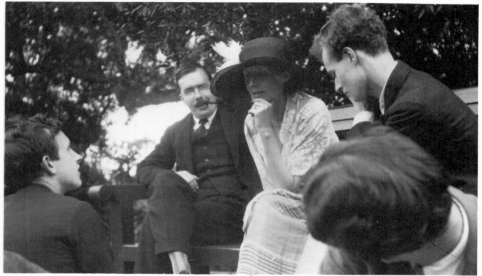

David Cecil, L. P. Hartley, Virginia Woolf, Anthony Asquith, and Sylvester Gates

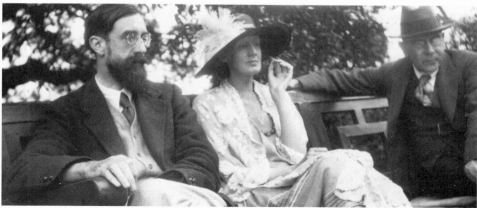

Lytton Strachey, Virginia Woolf, and G. Lowes Dickinson

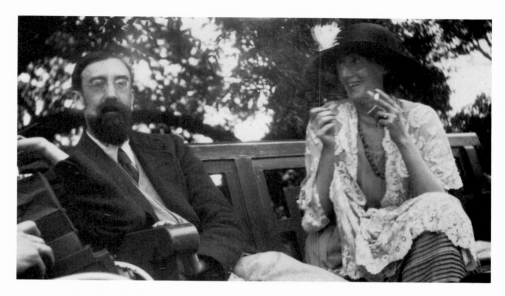

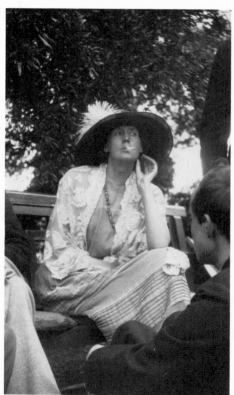

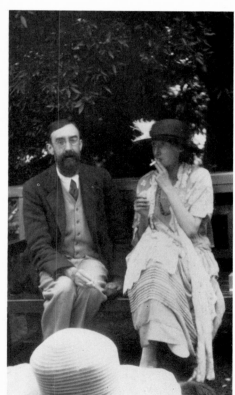

Was it wisdom? Was it knowledge? Was it, once more, the deceptiveness of beauty, so that all one's perceptions, half way to truth, were tangled in a golden mesh? or did she lock up within her some secret which certainly . . . people must have for the world to go on at all? Every one could not be as helter skelter, hand to mouth as she was. But if they knew, could they tell one what they knew?

—VIRGINIA WOOLF,
To the Lighthouse

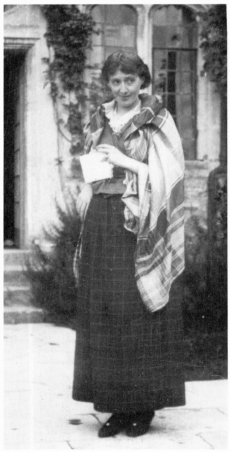 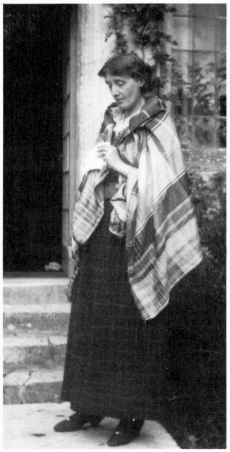

Virginia Woolf

"My dear boy," Le Chiffre spoke like a father, "the game of Red Indians is over, quite over. You have stumbled by chance into a game for grown-ups and you have already found it a painful experience. You are not equipped, my dear boy, to play games with adults, and it was very foolish of your nanny in London to have sent you out here with your spade and bucket. . . .

"Directly you left for the night club . . . your room was searched by four of my people. . . . We found a good deal in childish hiding-places. . . ."

—IAN FLEMING,
Casino Royale

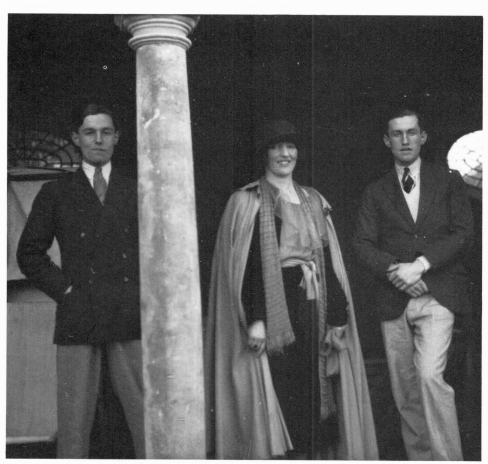

Mrs. Val Fleming with Ian and Peter Fleming at Garsington

. . . I had got a scholarship to Eton, from Eton to Balliol and from thence there would, I supposed, be other scholarships awaiting me; I could not imagine a moment when I should not be receiving marks for something, when "poor" or "very fair" or "Beta plus" was not being scrawled across my conduct-sheet by the Great Examiner. And yet already I was a defeatist, I remembered Teddy Jessel saying to me by the fives courts, in my hour of triumph: "Well, you've got a Balliol scholarship and you've got into Pop—you know I shouldn't be at all surprised if you never did anything else the rest of your life. After all, what happens to old tugs? If they're clever they become dons or civil servants, if not they come back here as ushers; when they're about forty they go to be with someone, if it's a boy they get sacked, if it's a woman they marry them. The pi ones go into the church and may become bishops. . . ." —CYRIL CONNOLLY, *Enemies of Promise*

Walter de la Mare and Cyril Connolly at Garsington, 1928

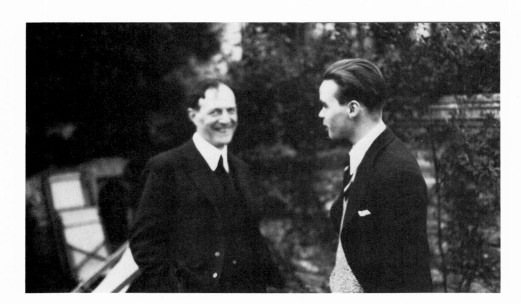

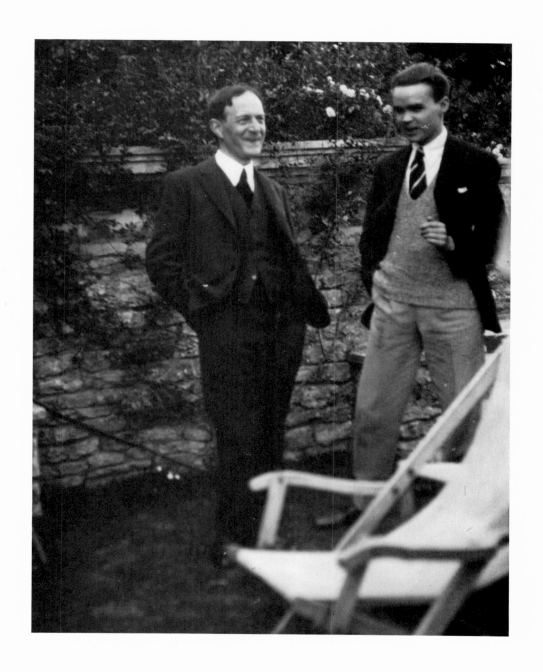

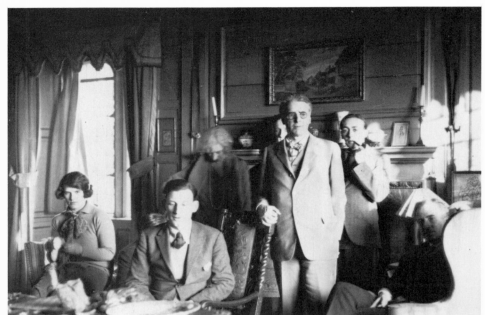

Julian Morrell, Siegfried Sassoon, Ethel Sands, W. B. Yeats, Eddy Sackville-West, and Philip Morrell

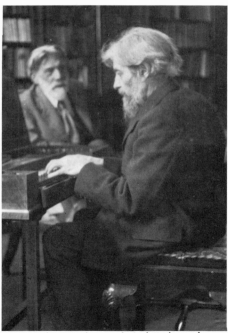

Robert Bridges and Carl Dolmetsch

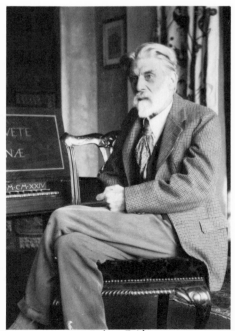

Robert Bridges

I have no more to give thee: lo, I have sold
My life, have emptied out my heart, and spent
Whate'er I had; till like a beggar, bold
With nought to lose, I laugh and am content.
A beggar kisses thee; nay, love, behold,
I fear not: thou art in beggarment.

     —ROBERT BRIDGES,
      "The Growth of Love"

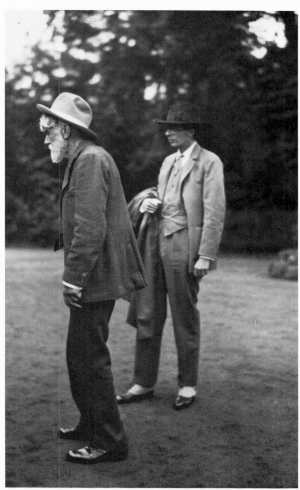

O weary pilgrims, chanting of your woe,
That turn your eyes to all the peaks that shine,
Hailing in each the citadel divine
The which ye thought to have entered long ago;
Until at length your feeble steps and slow
Falter upon the threshold of the shrine,
And your hearts overburdened doubt in fine
Whether it be Jerusalem or no:
Disheartened pilgrims, I am one of you;
For, having worshipped many a barren face,
I scarce now greet the goal I journeyed to;
I stand a pagan in the holy place;
Beneath the lamp of truth I am found untrue,
And question with the God that I embrace.

     —ROBERT BRIDGES,
      "The Growth of Love"

Robert Bridges and Aldous Huxley, 1928

. . . my brother and I understood her better than we would reveal. We understood her masculinity, her enduring regret that she was not born a boy, a boy who would have inherited Knole (Knole was like a lover to her, and that is why houses and the idea of inheritance play such an important part in her books), a boy who would have been sent to schools and a University, who would have learned Greek and Latin, and of whom it would have been assumed throughout his life that he could do things which girls could not do. She believed that she had to struggle for recognition more than a man. When a reviewer referred to her as an "authoress" or "poetess," she would raise her fists in the air with rage that was not diminished by our amusement. "If I'm anything," she expostulated, "I'm an *author*, a *poet*. Nobody ever talks about a 'gardeneress.' Why on earth, then, a 'poetess'?" Her strong masculinity came out in a number of ways: in her dislike of the institution (not the fact) of marriage, as if from that moment onwards the woman "belonged" to the man—she never introduced Harold Nicolson as "my husband," nor he her as "my wife" . . .

—NIGEL NICOLSON,
Introduction to *Harold Nicolson:
Diaries and Letters, 1930–1939*

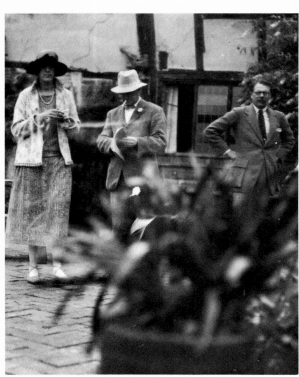

*Vita Sackville-West, Desmond MacCarthy,
and Harold Nicolson*

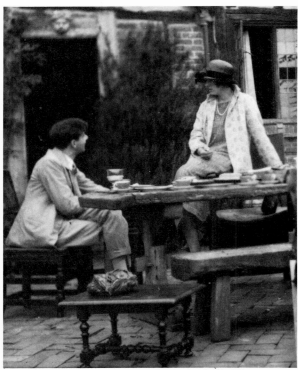

Raymond Mortimer and Vita Sackville-West

... They were not "her sort," they were often suspicious and stupid, and deficient where she excelled; but collision with them stimulated her, and she felt an interest that verged into liking. She desired to protect them, and often felt that they could protect her, excelling where she was deficient. Once past the rocks of emotion, they knew so well what to do, whom to send for; their hands were on all the ropes, they had grit as well as grittiness, and she valued grit enormously. They led a life that she could not attain to—the outer life of "telegrams and anger."

—E. M. FORSTER,
Howards End

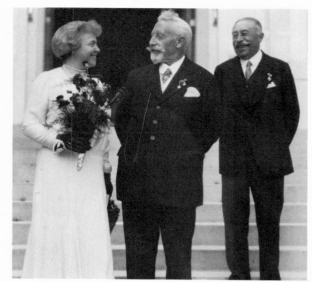

*Princess Cecilie, Kaiser Wilhelm II,
Count Godard Bentinck, at Amerongen in Holland*

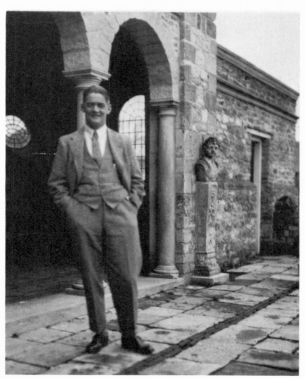

Lord Nuffield

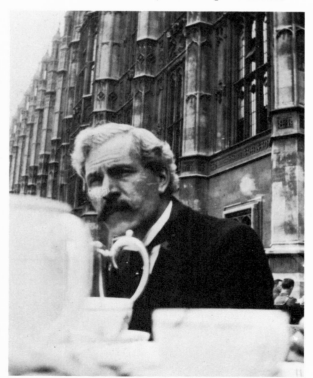

*Ramsay MacDonald
at the House of Commons*

As I climb I can talk aloud like the Heedless Blurter of China
Chanting without reserve my De Profundis of truth
Caring not if my voice has the major-tone or the minor,
Or if it murmurs in age what it should have shouted in youth—
Or if its tones resemble the leaves of a garden suburban
That refuses to sigh like a swamp, that refuses to roar like the sea
But insists that a man goes as mad in a bowler as under a turban
And that hearts that can bleed over wine can break over tea.

—JOHN COWPER POWYS,
"The Ridge"

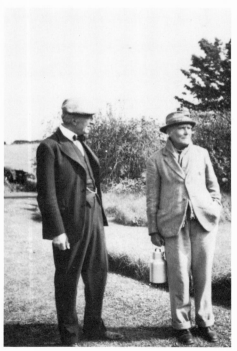

Philip Morrell and T. F. Powys, Dorset, 1924

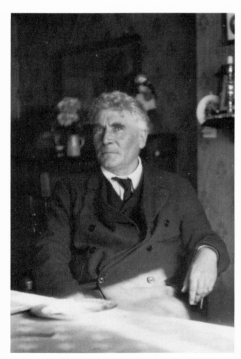

T. F. Powys, Dorset, 1924

Peter Ralli . . . came to New College with £3,000. During his three years he spent most of it, largely in giving delicious dinners, to which he often asked me. He had very black hair and a very pink face, and looked rather like an old-fashioned Dutch doll. He was wonderfully perceptive and entertaining, and a most rewarding waster of time. His chief energies were given to horse-racing, and he did no work at all. When he took History finals in 1922, he answered very few questions, and those briefly, one example being the single sentence, written in a huge, flowing hand, "Her subjects wanted Queen Elizabeth to abolish tunnage and poundage, but the splendid creature stood firm." He was, of course, ploughed, but it did not trouble him. After going down he was stricken by a long, incurable illness, and I used to visit him as he lay in bed. He was quite unchanged and never complained, but, being rather out of things, was avid for every kind of news. He made his nurse lay bets for him, and treated her with an intimate mockery which she adored but could not begin to understand. When he died, he had come to the end of his small fortune, from which he had derived and given enormous pleasure.

—C. M. BOWRA,
Memories, 1898–1939

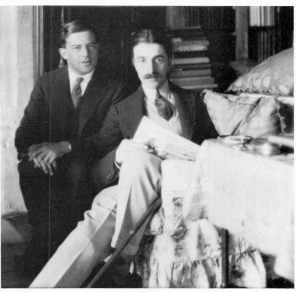

Maurice Bowra and Peter Ralli

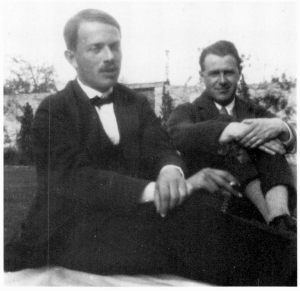

E. J. O'Brien and L. A. G. Strong at Garsington, 1924

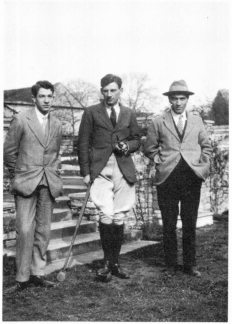

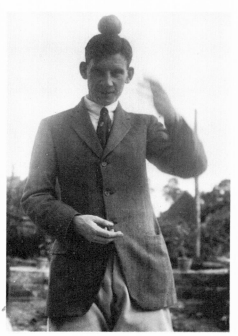

*Frank "Toronto" Prewett, Siegfried Sassoon,
and Colin de la Mare*

Siegfried Sassoon

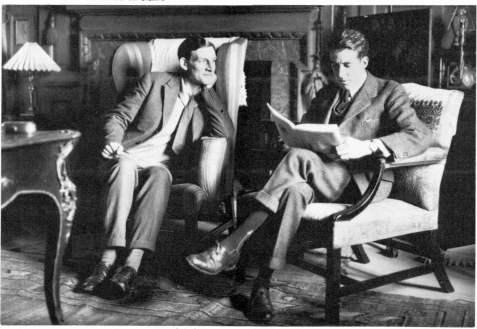

Siegfried Sassoon and W. J. Turner

In appearance he is tall, big-boned, loosely built. He is clean-shaven, pale or with a flush; has a heavy jaw, wide mouth with the upper lip slightly protruding and the curve of it very pronounced like that of a shrivelled leaf (as I have noticed is common in many poets). His nose is aquiline, the nostrils being wide and heavily arched. This characteristic and the fullness, depth and heat of his dark eyes give him the air of a sullen falcon. He speaks slowly, enunciating the words as if they pained him, in a voice that has something of the troubled thickness apparent in the voices of those who emerge from a deep grief. As he speaks, his large hands, roughened by trench toil and by riding, wander aimlessly until some emotion grips him when the knuckles harden and he clutches at his knees or at the edge of the table. And all the while he will be breathing hard like a man who has swum a distance. When he reads his poems he chants and one would think that he communed with himself save that, at the pauses, he shoots a powerful glance at the listener. Between the poems he is still but moves his lips. . . . He likes best to speak of hunting (he will shout of it!), of open air mornings when the gorse alone flames brighter than the sky, of country quiet, of his mother, of poetry—usually Shelley, Masefield and Thomas Hardy—and last and chiefly—but always with a rapid, tumbling enunciation and a much-irked desperate air filled with pain—of soldiers. For the incubus of war is on him so that his days are shot with anguish and his nights with horror. —ROBERT NICHOLS,

Introduction to Siegfried Sassoon, *Counter-Attack and Other Poems*

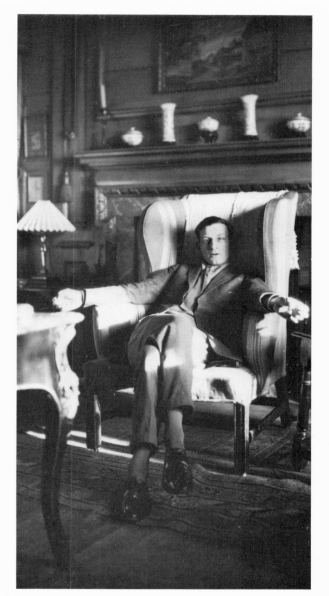

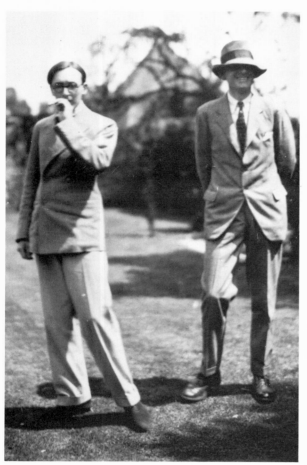

Eddy Sackville-West and Siegfried Sassoon

I find Siegfried very sympathetic and attractive, and my instinct goes out to him for he seems so intimate to me, as if he were a twin brother. He is natural and full of fun and perceptive of all things around. I find it a great joy to be with anyone so human and aware of ordinary life, after the intellectuals who walk along half-blind. Sometimes I feel that in him I have found that wonderful companion that I have so much desired, who would drink of the fountain of many colors that springs up in my inner self; but he is very aloof and obviously doesn't need my friendship. —*Ottoline at Garsington*

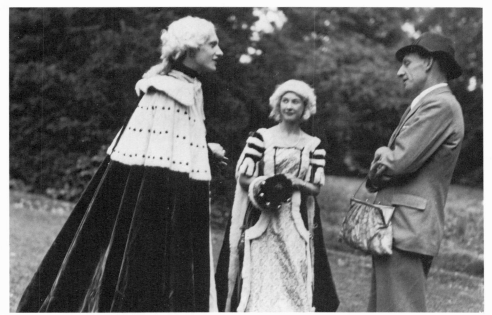

Lord David Cecil, Lady Cecil, and Siegfried Sassoon, Wilton, 1933

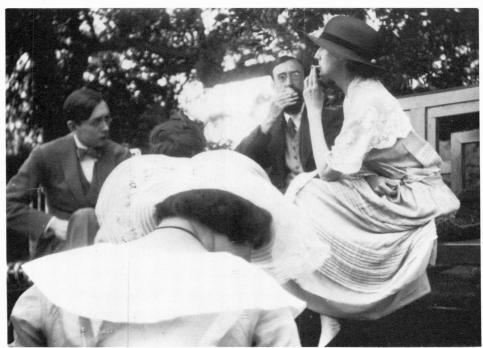

Eddy Sackville-West, Julian Morrell, Lytton Strachey, and Virginia Woolf

The tragedy of old age is not that one is old, but that one is young.

—OSCAR WILDE,
The Picture of Dorian Gray

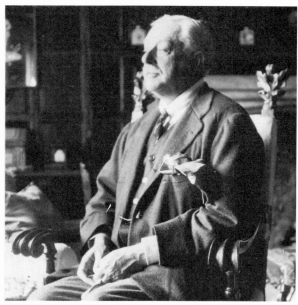

*Ottoline's half-brother,
the Sixth Duke of Portland, at Garsington*

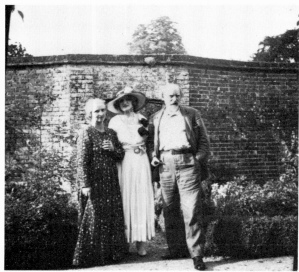

Dorelia and Augustus John with Ottoline, 1924

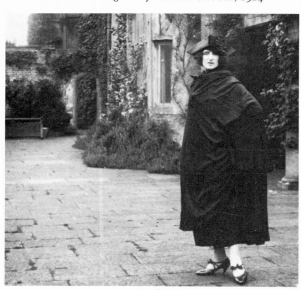

Ottoline

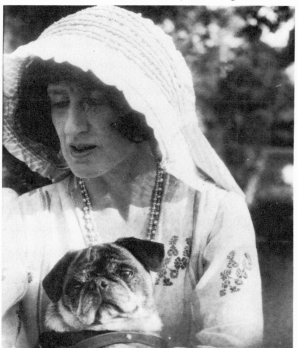

Ottoline with her pug dog Soie, about 1925

I think criticism imposed on him a tension very much like that imposed on the creator, but more painful because he had to deal with the work of others—and he was a man of extreme sensitivity as well as of ruthless honesty. In relation to me the literary critic had given way to the loving, contentious friend. No one has ever read my poems with more concentrated attention nor asked so much of me, but he stood *inside*, not *outside*. (His first wife had been Anne Douglas Sedgwick, and he was acutely aware of what it costs to be a woman and an artist.) Every writer needs one key person, one ear, one evaluator whom he can trust absolutely. There must be someone who registers triumphs with pure joy. Basil was that for me for more than twenty years.

. . . His was the most acute natural sensitivity I have ever known. He himself would have said it stemmed less from cultivation or instinct than from denying himself any stimulant whatever except tea. He neither drank nor smoked, and regarded any excess in such matters with visible distaste. He wanted, I think, to remain as naked a man as possible within a civilized society, to keep his senses as acute as an Indian's. This physical purity had something to do, no doubt, with his kind of perceptions as a literary critic.

—MAY SARTON
about Basil de Selincourt
in *Plant Dreaming Deep*

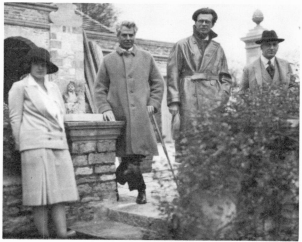

Julian Morrell, Basil de Selincourt,
Aldous Huxley, and Philip Morrell

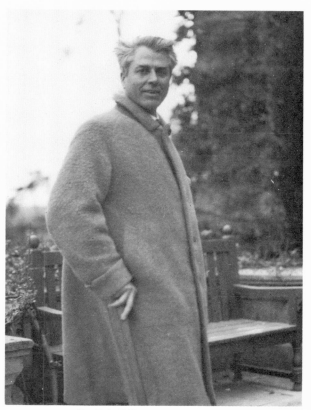

Basil de Selincourt at Garsington

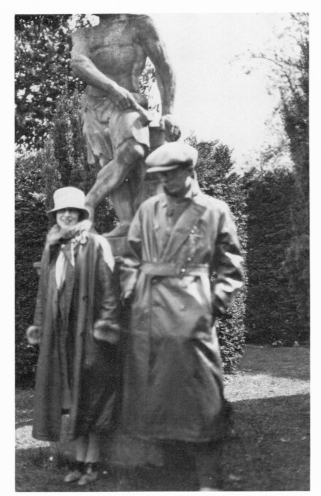
Aldous and Maria Huxley

. . . men are more solitary now than they were; all authority has gone; the tribe has disappeared and every at all conscious man stands alone, surrounded by other solitary individuals and fragments of the old tribe, for which he feels no respect. Obviously, the only thing to be done is to go right through with the process; to realize individuality to the full, the real individuality, Lao-Tze's individuality, the Yogis' individuality, and with it the oneness of everything. Obviously! But the difficulty is huge.

. . . And meanwhile the world is peopled with miserable beings who are neither one thing nor the other; who are solitary and yet not complete individuals. . . .

. . . What's to be done about it? That's the great question. Some day I may find some sort of answer. And then I may write a good book, or at any rate a mature book, not a queer sophisticatedly jejune book, like this last affair, like all the blooming lot, in fact.

—ALDOUS HUXLEY

in a letter to Robert Nichols, as quoted in Sybille Bedford, *Aldous Huxley*

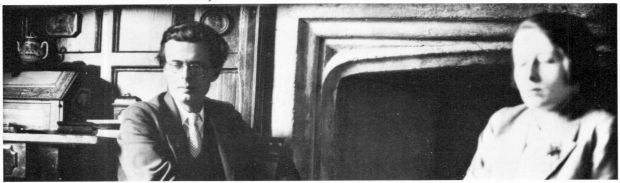

For a further two months after his return to England, Lytton was able to sample the pleasures of ordinary life. There were few notions of work, but plenty of social junketings. He dined with Somerset Maugham, and with Lady Cunard, Desmond MacCarthy and Noël Coward. He met William Gerhardie and Victor Cazalet at a party given by Syrie Maugham in the King's Road, and Charlie Chaplin at one of Ottoline's Gower Street receptions. . . .

This exhaustion, which came over him very easily now, he put down to "too much wit and too little humour perhaps." Even so, despite feeling drained of all energy, he was suffering from a restless sense of impatience—"one of the worst cares of life!" He had little wish to work, but an overpowering urge to enjoy himself, and he rushed up to the idle and idyllic whirl of London. Dining with Clive Bell one evening shortly after arriving in Gordon Square, he complained of feeling off colour, and left early, saying that they must meet again soon when he was well. The following Friday they dined once more. This time he appeared to be better, and Clive Bell "enjoyed one of those evenings which Lytton contrived to turn into works of art." The next day, Saturday, accompanied by Pippa and some other relatives, he travelled down by train to Ham Spray. At Paddington he discovered by chance that Clive Bell was journeying to Wiltshire in the same coach. "He came to see me in my compartment," Clive Bell recorded, "where I was alone, and we had some talk, mostly about my tussle with the Commissioners of Inland Revenue, who, as usual, were behaving disagreeably. At Reading he rejoined his party. At Hungerford I watched him walk along the platform on his way out. That was the last time I saw Lytton."

—MICHAEL HOLROYD,
Lytton Strachey

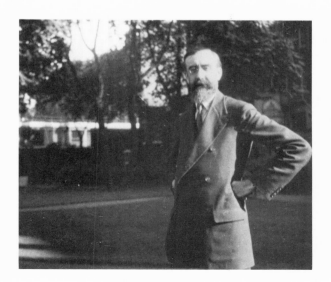

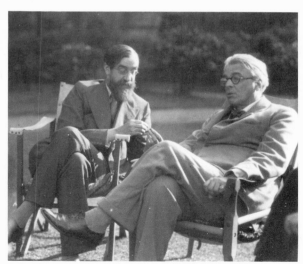

Strachey and W. B. Yeats at Gower Street

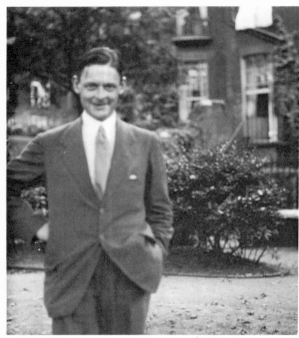

T. S. Eliot at Gower Street, about 1928

We are in many ways in a position of advantage over our mediaeval ancestors. We are more humane, cleaner, and have better table manners; we may be less saintly than some, but we are less beastly than others; we have material comforts, hygiene, machinery and invention, which we do not wish to dispense with but to manipulate wisely. —T. S. ELIOT,

"Christianity and Communism"

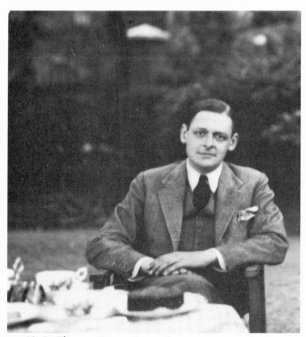

T. S. Eliot at Gower Street, between 1932 and 1934

When Lawrence was dead and I was in London I went to see her and had forgotten it was her "Thursday." Her maid that I remembered announced me to the people having tea in the dining-room. "Mrs. D. H. Lawrence." For a few seconds there was absolute silence. Then they got up and talked to me. And after a little while Ottoline took me aside and said in her strange voice: "Frieda, I must tell you that I never was fair to you." She had sent Bertie R. to tell Lawrence that he must get rid of me. I think England never liked me, not for a minute. But Ottoline was no small beer. The English are too English, like ingrown toenails.

—FRIEDA LAWRENCE:
The Memoirs and Correspondence

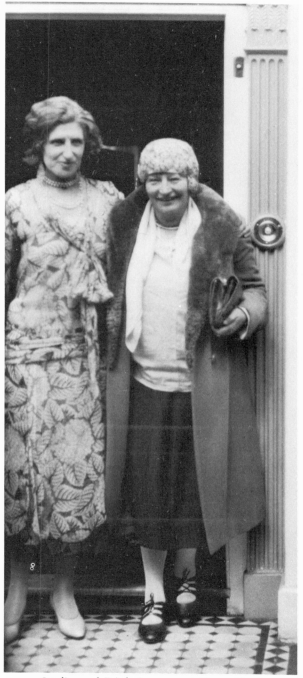

Ottoline and Frieda Lawrence at Gower Street

There were also teas on days other than Thursdays, for smaller groups. On one of these occasions I was invited to meet W. B. Yeats. Yeats, at the age of seventy, had something of the appearance of an overgrown art student, with shaggy, hanging head and a dazed, gray, blind gaze. On the occasion of our first meeting he looked at me fixedly and said: "What, young man, do you think of the Sayers?" This took me aback and I murmured that I had not read any. "The Sayers," he repeated, "the Sayers." Lady Ottoline then explained that he was speaking of a certain troupe of speakers who recited poetry in chorus. I knew even less of these than of detective fiction and had to admit so. Lady Ottoline, who had arranged for us to have tea with very few people present, saw that I was a failure. She left the room and telephoned to Virginia Woolf to get into a taxi and come round from Tavistock Square *at once*. Virginia, highly amused, arrived a few minutes later.

After tea, I listened, relieved not to have to take part in the conversation, while Yeats sat on the sofa with Virginia Woolf and explained to her that her novel, *The Waves*, expressed in fiction the idea of pulsations of energy throughout the universe which was common to the modern theories of physicists and to recent discoveries in psychic research. —STEPHEN SPENDER,
World Within World

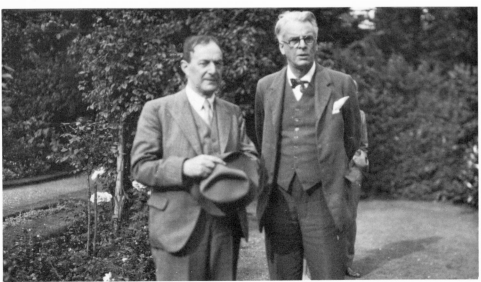

Walter de la Mare and W. B. Yeats, Taplow, about 1935

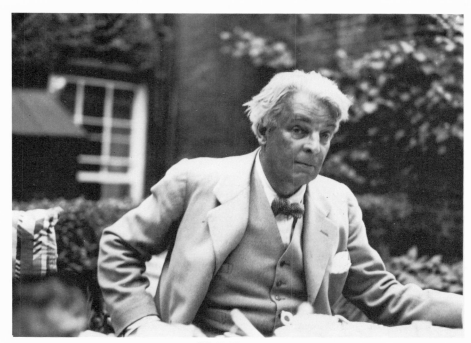

W. B. Yeats, 1935

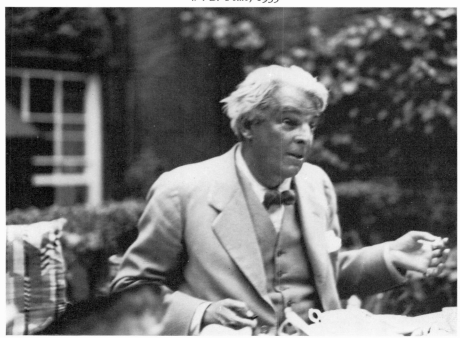

Desmond [MacCarthy], in the imagination of his friends, was going to be the successor of Henry James. Hearing him talk you could believe that. Even when he had sunk beneath repeated failures to float magazines, to produce copy on time, to meet the demands of bailiffs, to cope with life at all, still he had only to speak in order to command, not so much attention as affection, to fill one with delight, and, when he was in the vein, to convince one that he was the master of some prodigious treasury. He had only to put his hand into his pocket and draw out whatever you might wish—subtlety, brilliance or deep imaginative richness. It was "ask and have," for he was the most carelessly generous, the most intellectually spendthrift of men. How few plays have ever enchanted one half so much as Desmond's small talk.

—QUENTIN BELL,
Virginia Woolf

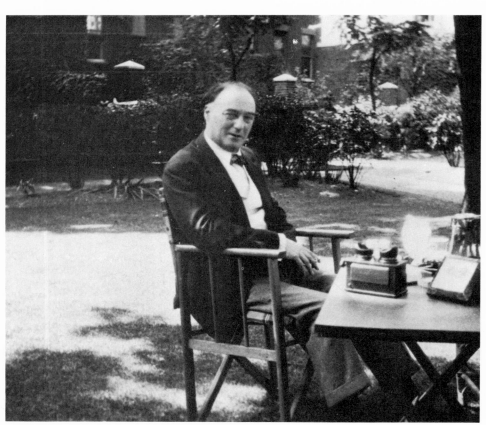

Sir Desmond MacCarthy at Gower Street

I found in Juliette and Julian Huxley a grace, a charm, a way of making a stranger feel at home that melts that first occasion into many others, and into years of friendship. What I do remember was my delight in observing them together, for they would take almost any odd scrap of information or opinion and toss it agilely to each other like a ping-pong ball, an airy, teasing game, punctuated by bursts of laughter, until Juliette after a particularly daring sally, put her hands to her face and said, "I have shocked myself."

—MAY SARTON,
I Knew a Phoenix

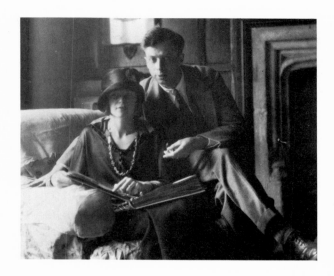

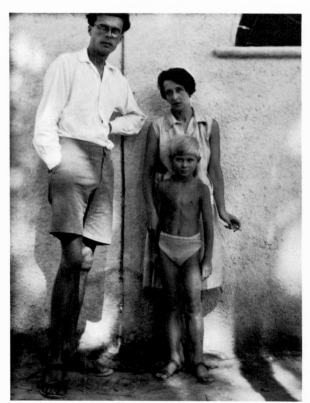

Aldous and Maria Huxley with their son Matthew in Italy

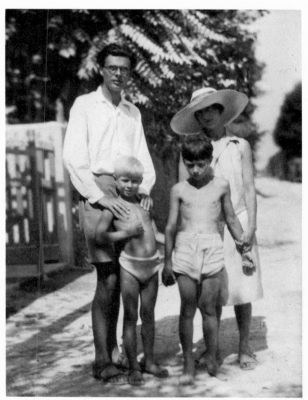

*The Aldous Huxleys.
The other child may be Julian Huxley's son.*

One evening my concierge told me as I came in that a tall, beautiful, blind gentleman had called and had left a note for me. It was from Joyce, and it asked me to meet him the next day. After that we met several times a week for a long time. I discovered that he approved of me in the most astonishing fashion, but it took me a little time to find out why. Then as the Dublin newsboys used to yell at customers, the whole discovery was found out.

How Joyce had made this discovery, I don't know, but he revealed to me that his name was James and mine was James, that my name was Stephens, and the name he had taken for himself in his best book was Stephen: that he and I were born in the same country, in the same city, in the same year, in the same month, on the same day, at the same hour, six o'clock in the morning on the second of February. He held, with a certain contained passion, that the second of February, his day and my day, was the day of the bear, the badger and the boar. On the second of February the squirrel lifts his nose out of his tail and surmises lovingly of nuts, the bee blinks and thinks again of the Sleeping Beauty, his queen, the wasp rasps and rustles and thinks that he is Napoleon Bonaparte, the robin twitters and thinks of love and worms. I learned that on that day of days Joyce and I, Adam and Eve, Dublin and the Devil all shake a leg and come a-popping and a-hopping yelling here we are again, we and the world and the moon are new, up the poets, up the rabbits and the spiders and the rats.

Well, I was astonished. I was admired at last. Joyce admired me. I was beloved at last: Joyce loved me. Or did he? Or did he only love his birthday, and was I merely coincident to that? When I spoke about my verse, which was every waking minute of my time, Joyce listened heartily and said "Ah." He approved of it as second of February verse, but I'm not certain that he really considered it to be better than the verse of Shakespeare and Racine and Dante. And yet he knew the verse of those three exhaustively!

Now in order to bring this birthday to an end, let's do it in the proper way. If I were Joyce's twin, which he held, then I had to celebrate this astonishing fact in my own way. So upon our next birthday I sent him a small poem. . . . Joyce reported back to me that he was much obliged. He practically said "Ah" to my poem ["Sarasvata"], and I could almost see him rubbing his chin at it.

—JAMES STEPHENS,
as quoted in Richard Ellmann,
James Joyce

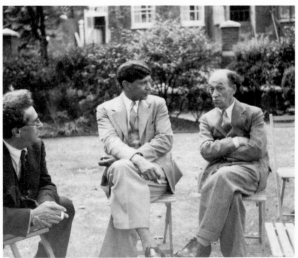

*S. S. Koteliansky, Bosie Sen,
and James Stephens at Gower Street*

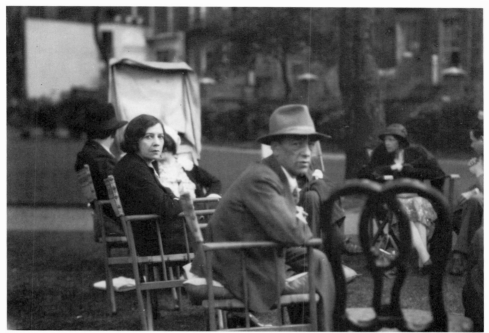

Vivienne Eliot and James Stephens at Gower Street, 1932

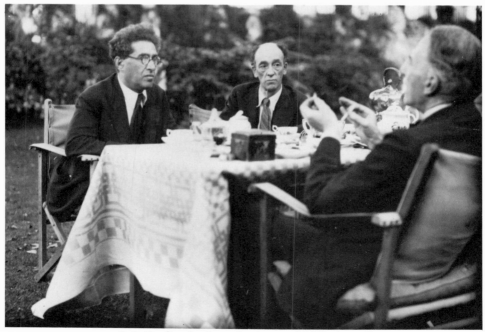

S. S. Koteliansky, James Stephens, and Philip Morrell

Her style is a writer's delight, there is an enjoyment of the grotesque, of absurd conversations as between Dublin ladies straight out of Congreve, a passionate sense of place, of love affairs, the interior decoration of not so humble homes, flashes of observation as of the Anglo-Irish lady tapping the turf fire with her brocaded evening slipper. She was the intellectual peer of her friends Virginia Woolf and Edith Sitwell, a poet content to work her imagination into the texture of her prose. —CYRIL CONNOLLY,

as quoted in the Foreword to

Elizabeth Bowen, *Pictures and Conversations*

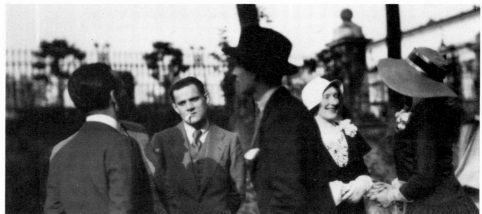

Alberto Moravia (with cigarette), Lord David Cecil, Elizabeth Bowen, and Ottoline

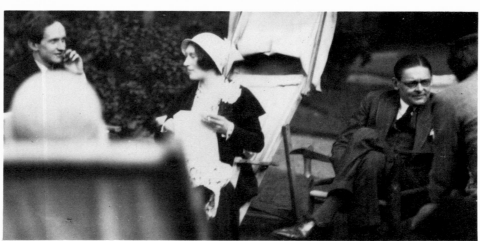

Lord David Cecil, Elizabeth Bowen, and T. S. Eliot at Gower Street, 1932

"He was like his beautiful face; a prophet, a seer, a boy, and a kindly jester," Copley wrote in one of the tributes collected by Sturge Moore's widow. The kindly jester is not apparent in the poet's works, which contain only the mild humor of a few sporadic puns, but men and women who knew him attest to his whimsicality and drollery in everyday life. Edith Cooper set him off in this respect against Yeats, whose wit, she said, was "rhetorical—not the instinctive mischief and drollery, the moment's wild happiness in some contrast, that is so engaging in Tommy." Even an American, Ferris Greenslet, who attended a luncheon which Edmund Gosse gave at the House of Lords for Barrie, Noyes, "and the woolly-bearded poet, Sturge Moore," colorfully substantiates Copley's picture: "As Moore entered late, Gosse, a naughty host, whispered in my ear, 'A sheep in sheep's clothing.' But as the talk rose on the tide of the House's admirable cellar, the sheep proved the life of the party."

—FREDERICK L. GWYNN,
Sturge Moore and the Life of Art

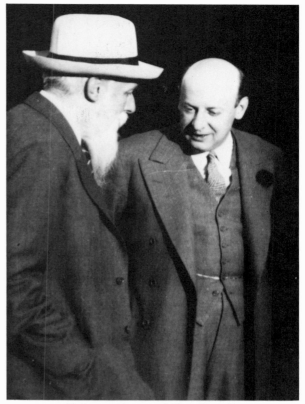

T. Sturge Moore and Marc Connelly

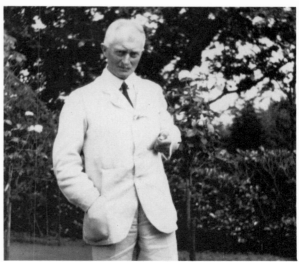

John Masefield at Boar's Hill, about 1935

. . . I felt that Rosamond had established novels as her territory in a way that I could never possibly rival. It was not only my own admiration for her books that taught me that; but her fans and fan-mail, in which letters of perceptive, heart-warming praise from shrewd critics were mixed up with bedlamite outpourings of hysteria, reckless intimate confidences from unknown pilgrims of eternity of both sexes, proposals of marriage from the Colonies, unsolicited illegible manuscripts from aspiring authors who saw her as soulmate and star disclosed by Heaven to guide them, demands for immediate cash support and love-sonnets from remote Alpine monasteries. —JOHN LEHMANN, *In My Own Time*

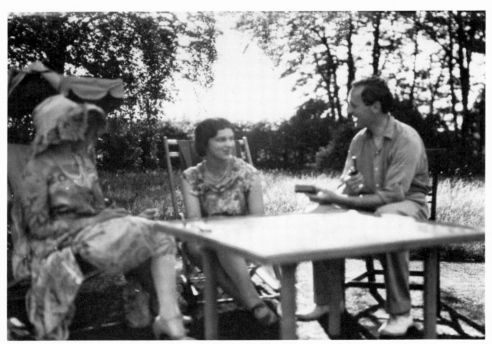

Ottoline, Rosamond Lehmann, and Wogan Philipps

Ottoline's burial service. Oh dear, oh dear the lack of intensity; the wailing and mumbling; the fumbling with bags; the shuffling; the vast brown mass of respectable old South Kensington ladies. And then the hymns; and the clergyman with a bar of medals across his surplice; and the orange and blue windows; and a toy Union Jack sticking from a cranny. What had all this to do with Ottoline, or our feelings? Save that the address was to the point: a critical study, written presumably by Philip and delivered, very resonantly, by Mr. Speaight the actor: a sober, and secular speech, which made one at least think of a human being, though the reference to her beautiful voice caused one to think of that queer nasal moan: however that too was to the good in deflating immensities. —VIRGINIA WOOLF,
A Writer's Diary,
Tuesday, April 26, 1938

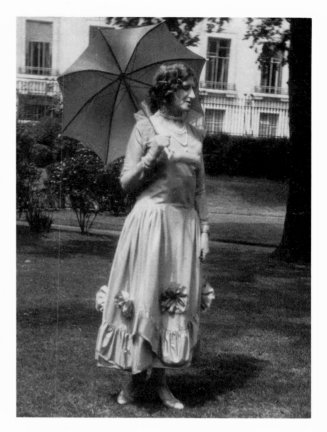

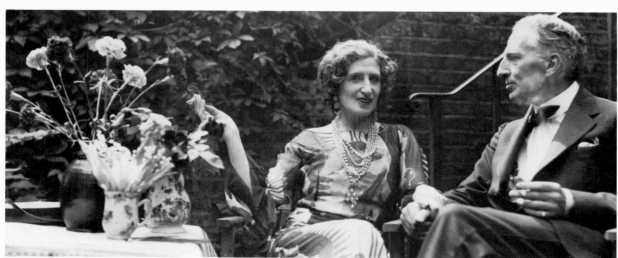

Ottoline and Philip, June 16, 1935

SOURCE NOTES

17 *Memoirs of Lady Ottoline Morrell: A Study in Friendship, 1873–1915,* edited by Robert Gathorne-Hardy (Alfred A. Knopf, 1964; Faber and Faber), pp. 3–4.

18 C. M. Bowra, *Memories, 1898–1939* (Harvard University Press, 1966; Weidenfeld and Nicolson), p. 194.

19 William Plomer, *At Home* (Farrar, Straus & Giroux, 1958; Jonathan Cape), pp. 50–51.

20 *Memoirs of Lady Ottoline Morrell,* pp. 72, 74.

22 Trevor Wilson, *The Downfall of the Liberal Party, 1914–1935* (Cornell University Press, 1966; William Collins Sons), pp. 31, 34.

24 D. H. Lawrence, *Women in Love* (Viking Press; The Hogarth Press).

26 *Memoirs of Lady Ottoline Morrell,* pp. 46–47.

30 David Gadd, *The Loving Friends: A Portrait of Bloomsbury* (Harcourt Brace Jovanovich, 1975; The Hogarth Press), p. 65.

32 Kenneth Clark, "A Peer Gynt from the Slade," *Times Literary Supplement* (October 18, 1974).

36 *Memoirs of Lady Ottoline Morrell,* pp. 109–110, 112.

38 *The Autobiography of Bertrand Russell,* 2 vols. (Little, Brown, 1967, 1968; George Allen & Unwin), Vol. I, p. 274.

41 Leon Edel, *Henry James: The Master, 1901–1916* (J. B. Lippincott, 1972; Rupert Hart Davis), p. 480.

42 Michael Holroyd, *Lytton Strachey: A Critical Biography,* 2 vols. (Holt, Rinehart, 1968; William Heinemann, 1967, 1968), Vol. II, pp. 57–58.

44 Siegfried Sassoon, *Siegfried's Journey* (Viking Press, 1946; Faber and Faber), p. 12.

46 William Butler Yeats, "Meditations in Time of Civil War," from *The Collected Poems of W. B. Yeats* (New York: Macmillan, 1956; London and Basingstoke: Macmillan), pp. 198–199.

48 David Garnett, *The Flowers of the Forest* (Harcourt Brace Jovanovich, 1955; Chatto & Windus), pp. 108–109.

50 John Woodeson, *Mark Gertler* (University of Toronto Press, 1973; Sidgwick & Jackson), p. 258.

52 Sybille Bedford, *Aldous Huxley* (Alfred A. Knopf/Harper & Row, 1974; Chatto & Windus/William Collins Sons, 1973), p. 72.

53 *The Collected Letters of D. H. Lawrence,* 2 vols., edited by Harry T. Moore (Viking Press, 1962; William Heinemann), Vol. I, p. 401.

54 Aldous Huxley, *Point Counter Point* (Harper & Row, 1928; Chatto & Windus), pp. 97–98.

54 *The Letters of Katherine Mansfield,* 2 vols., edited by J. Middleton Murry (Alfred A. Knopf, 1929; Constable), Vol. I, p. 191.

55 Naomi Mitchison, in *Aldous Huxley Memorial Volume,* edited by Julian Huxley (Harper & Row, 1965; Chatto & Windus), pp. 52–53.

56 *Letters of Katherine Mansfield,* Vol. I, p. 182.

58 Garnett, *Flowers,* p. 150.

60 Russell, *Autobiography,* Vol. II, p. 130.

61 W. H. Auden, "A Literary Transference," *The Southern Review,* Vol. VI (1940), 139–140.

62 E. M. Forster, *Two Cheers for Democracy* (Edward Arnold Publishers, 1951; reprinted by Harcourt Brace Jovanovich, 1962), pp. 232–233.

63 Holroyd, *Strachey,* Vol. II, p. 334.

64 P. N. Furbank, "The Personality of E. M. Forster," *Encounter* (November, 1970), p. 61.

64 J. R. Ackerley, *E. M. Forster: A Portrait* (Ian McKelvie, 1970), pp. 20–22.

66 Yeats, *Collected Poems*, p. 204.

67 Woodeson, *Gertler*, p. 7.

68 Robert Graves, *Good-bye to All That* (Doubleday Anchor Books, 1957; Eyre Methuen).

70 T. S. Eliot, *Collected Poems, 1909–1962* (Harcourt Brace Jovanovich, 1943).

73 William Plomer, "Recollections of Virginia Woolf," in *Recollections of Virginia Woolf*, edited by Joan Russell Noble (William Morrow; Peter Owen, 1952), p. 107.

76 Virginia Woolf, Lady Ottoline Morrell obituary, London *Times*, April 28, 1938.

78 Clive Bell, *Old Friends* (Chatto & Windus, 1956; reprinted by University of Chicago Press, 1973), p. 118.

80 Virginia Woolf, *To the Lighthouse* (Harcourt Brace Jovanovich, 1927, 1949; The Hogarth Press), p. 78.

81 Ian Fleming, *Casino Royale* (New York: Macmillan, 1953; Jonathan Cape).

82 Cyril Connolly, *Enemies of Promise* (New York: Macmillan, 1948; Routledge & Kegan Paul), pp. 252–253.

85 Robert Bridges, "The Growth of Love," from *The Poetical Works of Robert Bridges* (New York: Macmillan; Oxford: Oxford University Press).

86 Nigel Nicolson, Introduction to *Harold Nicolson: Diaries and Letters, 1930–1939* (Atheneum, 1966; William Collins Sons), pp. 17–18.

87 E. M. Forster, *Howards End* (Alfred A. Knopf, 1921; Edward Arnold Publishers).

88 John Cowper Powys, "The Ridge," in *A Review of English Literature* (January, 1963).

89 Bowra, *Memories*, p. 123.

91 Robert Nichols, Introduction to Siegfried Sassoon, *Counter-Attack and Other Poems* (E. P. Dutton, 1918; William Heinemann), pp. 1–2.

92 *Ottoline at Garsington: Memoirs of Lady Ottoline Morrell, 1915–1918*, edited by Robert Gathorne-Hardy (Alfred A. Knopf, 1975; Faber and Faber), p. 152.

94 Oscar Wilde, *The Picture of Dorian Gray*, edited by Isobel M. Murray (Oxford University Press, 1974).

95 May Sarton, *Plant Dreaming Deep* (W. W. Norton, 1968), pp. 158–159.

96 Bedford, *Huxley*, p. 159.

97 Holroyd, *Strachey*, Vol. II, pp. 695–697.

98 T. S. Eliot, "Christianity and Communism," *The Listener* (March 16, 1932), p. 383.

99 *Frieda Lawrence: The Memoirs and Correspondence*, edited by E. W. Tedlock, Jr. (Alfred A. Knopf, 1964; William Heinemann), p. 390.

100 *World Within World: The Autobiography of Stephen Spender* (University of California Press, 1951), pp. 148–149.

102 Quentin Bell, *Virginia Woolf: A Biography*, 2 vols. (Harcourt Brace Jovanovich, 1972; The Hogarth Press), Vol. II, p. 82.

103 May Sarton, *I Knew a Phoenix* (W. W. Norton, 1954; Peter Owen), p. 206.

104 James Stephens, as quoted in Richard Ellmann, *James Joyce* (New York and Oxford: Oxford University Press, 1959), pp. 605–606. Footnoted as "The James Joyce I Knew," *The Listener*, Vol. XXXVI (October 24, 1946), p. 566.

106 Cyril Connolly, Foreword to Elizabeth Bowen, *Pictures and Conversations* (Alfred A. Knopf, 1975; Allen Lane), p. xii.

107 Frederick L. Gwynn, *Sturge Moore and the Life of Art* (Folcroft Library editions, 1973), pp. 73–74.

108 John Lehmann, *In My Own Time* (Atlantic/Little, Brown, 1969), p. 84.

109 *A Writer's Diary: Being Extracts from the Diary of Virginia Woolf*, edited by Leonard Woolf (Harcourt Brace Jovanovich, 1953; The Hogarth Press), p. 280.

INDEX

—◆❦◆—

Note: Page numbers in italics refer to illustrations.

PERMISSIONS ACKNOWLEDGMENTS

Grateful acknowledgment is made to the following for permission to reprint previously published material:

17, Alfred A. Knopf, Inc., and Faber & Faber Ltd.: For
20, excerpts from *Memoirs of Lady Ottoline Morrell: A*
26, *Study in Friendship, 1873–1915*, edited by Robert Ga-
36 thorne-Hardy. Copyright © 1963 by Julian Vinogradoff.

18, Harvard University Press and Weidenfeld & Nicolson:
89 For excerpts from *Memories, 1898–1939*, by C. Maurice
Bowra. Published in 1966.

19 Jonathan Cape Ltd. on behalf of the Estate of William
Plomer: For an excerpt from *At Home*, by William
Plomer. Published in 1958.

22 William Collins Sons and Co. Ltd.: For an excerpt from
The Downfall of the Liberal Party, 1914–1935, by Trevor
Wilson. Published in 1966.

24 The Viking Press, Inc., Laurence Pollinger Ltd., and
the Estate of the late Mrs. Frieda Lawrence: For an
excerpt from *Women in Love*, by D. H. Lawrence. Copyright 1920, 1922 by D. H. Lawrence, renewed 1948, 1950
by Frieda Lawrence. All rights reserved.

30 Harcourt Brace Jovanovich, Inc., and The Hogarth Press
Ltd.: For an excerpt from *The Loving Friends*, by David
Gadd. Published in 1975.

32 Lord Clark and the *Times Literary Supplement*: For an
excerpt from "A Peer Gynt from the Slade," by Kenneth
Clark, which appeared in the *Supplement* of October 18,
1974.

38, Little, Brown and Company and George Allen & Unwin
60 Ltd.: For excerpts from *The Autobiography of Bertrand
Russell*, Vols. I and II. Published in 1967 and 1968.

41 J. B. Lippincott Company and William Morris Agency,
Inc., as agents for Leon Edel: For an excerpt from *Henry
James: The Master, 1901–1916*, by Leon Edel. Copy-
right © 1972 by Leon Edel.

42, Holt, Rinehart & Winston, Inc., and William Heine-
63, mann Ltd.: For excerpts from *Lytton Strachey*, by Michael
97 Holroyd. Copyright © 1968 by Michael Holroyd.

44 The Viking Press, Inc., and Mr. George T. Sassoon: For
an excerpt from *Siegfried's Journey*, by Siegfried Sassoon.
Copyright 1945 by Siegfried Sassoon, renewed 1973 by
George T. Sassoon. All rights reserved.

46, Macmillan Publishing Co., Inc., and M. B. Yeats, Miss
66 Anne Yeats, and Macmillan of London & Basingstoke:
For sixteen lines of "Meditations in Time of Civil War,"
from *The Collected Poems of W. B. Yeats*. Copyright

1928 by Macmillan Publishing Co., Inc., renewed 1956
by George Yeats.

48, Harcourt Brace Jovanovich, Inc., and Chatto & Windus
58 Ltd.: For excerpts from *The Flowers of the Forest*, by
David Garnett. Copyright © 1955 by David Garnett.

50, University of Toronto Press and Sidgwick & Jackson Ltd.:
67 For excerpts from *Mark Gertler*, by John Woodeson.
Published in 1973.

52, Alfred A. Knopf, Inc., Dr. Jan Van Loewen Ltd., and
96 the Estate of Aldous Huxley: For excerpts from *Aldous
Huxley*, by Sybille Bedford. Copyright © 1973, 1974 by
Sybille Bedford.

53 The Viking Press, Inc., Laurence Pollinger Ltd., and the
Estate of the late Mrs. Frieda Lawrence: For an excerpt
from *The Collected Letters of D. H. Lawrence*, edited
by Harry T. Moore. Copyright © 1962 by Angelo
Ravagli and C. M. Weekley, Executors of the Estate of
Frieda Lawrence Ravagli. All rights reserved.

54 Harper & Row Publishers, Inc., Chatto & Windus Ltd.,
and Mrs. Laura Huxley: For an excerpt from *Point
Counter Point*, by Aldous Huxley. Published in 1928.

54, Alfred A. Knopf, Inc., and The Society of Authors as the
56 literary representative of the Estate of Katherine Mansfield: For excerpts from *The Letters of Katherine
Mansfield*, edited by John Middleton Murry. Copyright
1928, 1929 by Alfred A. Knopf, Inc., renewed 1956,
1957 by John Middleton Murry.

55 Chatto & Windus Ltd. and the Literary Estate of Julian
Huxley: For excerpts by Naomi Mitchison from *Aldous
Huxley, 1894–1963: A Memorial Volume*, edited by
Julian Huxley. Published by Harper & Row, 1965.

61 Louisiana State University: For an excerpt from "A
Literary Transference," by W. H. Auden, in *Hardy:
A Collection of Critical Essays*, edited by Albert J.
Guerard. Copyright 1940, 1941 by Louisiana State Uni-
versity. Originally appeared in *The Southern Review*,
vol. VI, 1940.

62 Harcourt Brace Jovanovich, Inc., and Edward Arnold
(Publishers) Ltd.: For an excerpt from *Two Cheers for
Democracy*, by E. M. Forster. Copyright 1951 by E. M.
Forster.

64 *Encounter*: Excerpt from "The Personality of E. M.
Forster," by P. N. Furbank. Reprinted from *Encounter*,
November, 1970, issue.

64 David Higham Associates Ltd.: For an excerpt from *E. M. Forster: A Portrait*, by J. R. Ackerley. Published in 1970 by Ian McKelvie Ltd.

68 Collins-Knowlton-Wing: For an excerpt from *Good-bye to All That*, by Robert Graves. Copyright 1929, © 1957 by Robert Graves. Published by Doubleday Anchor Books.

70 Harcourt Brace Jovanovich, Inc., Faber & Faber Ltd., and Mrs. T. S. Eliot: For lines from "East Coker," in *Collected Poems, 1909–1962*, by T. S. Eliot. Copyright 1943 by T. S. Eliot, copyright renewed 1971 by Esme Valerie Eliot.

73 William Morrow & Co. and Peter Owen Ltd.: For an excerpt by William Plomer from *Recollections of Virginia Woolf*, edited by Joan Russell Noble. Published in 1952.

76 The Hogarth Press Ltd. and the Literary Estate of Virginia Woolf: For an excerpt from the obituary for Lady Ottoline Morrell which appeared in *The Times* (London) April 28, 1938.

78 University of Chicago Press and Chatto & Windus Ltd.: For an excerpt from *Old Friends*, by Clive Bell. Published by Chatto & Windus, 1956; University of Chicago Press, 1973.

80 Harcourt Brace Jovanovich, Inc., The Hogarth Press Ltd., and the Literary Estate of Virginia Woolf: For an excerpt from *To the Lighthouse*, by Virginia Woolf. Copyright 1927 by Harcourt Brace Jovanovich, Inc., renewed 1955 by Leonard Woolf.

81 Macmillan Publishing Co., Inc., and Glidrose Publications Ltd.: For an excerpt from *Casino Royale*, by Ian Fleming. Copyright 1953, 1954 by Glidrose Publications Ltd.

82 David Higham Associates Ltd.: For an excerpt from *Enemies of Promise*, by Cyril Connolly. Published by Routledge & Kegan Paul Ltd.

85 Oxford University Press (Oxford, England): For excerpts from "The Growth of Love," from *The Poetical Works of Robert Bridges*.

86 Atheneum Publishers, Inc., and William Collins Sons and Co. Ltd.: For an excerpt from *Harold Nicolson: Diaries and Letters, 1930–1939*, edited by Nigel Nicolson. Copyright © 1966, 1967 by William Collins Sons and Co. Ltd.

87 Alfred A. Knopf, Inc., and Edward Arnold (Publishers) Ltd.: For an excerpt from *Howards End*, by E. M. Forster. Copyright 1921 by E. M. Forster.

88 Laurence Pollinger Ltd. on behalf of the Estate of the late John Cowper Powys: For eight lines from "The Ridge," by John Cowper Powys. Reprinted from *A Review of English Literature*, January, 1963.

91 Hope Leresche & Steele: For an excerpt from the Introduction by Robert Nichols to *Counter-Attack and Other Poems*, by Siegfried Sassoon. Copyright 1918 by Robert Nichols.

92 Alfred A. Knopf, Inc., and Faber & Faber Ltd.: For an excerpt from *Ottoline at Garsington: Memoirs of Lady Ottoline Morrell, 1915–1918*, edited by Robert Gathorne-Hardy. Copyright © 1974 by Julian Vinogradoff.

95 W. W. Norton & Company, Inc., and Russell & Volkening, Inc.: For an excerpt from *Plant Dreaming Deep,* by May Sarton. Copyright © 1968 by May Sarton.

98 Faber & Faber Ltd. and Mrs. T. S. Eliot: For an excerpt from "Christianity and Communism," by T. S. Eliot, from *The Listener*, March 16, 1932. Copyright 1932 by T. S. Eliot.

99 Alfred A. Knopf, Inc., Laurence Pollinger Ltd., and the Estate of the late Mrs. Frieda Lawrence: For an excerpt from *Frieda Lawrence: The Memoirs and Correspondence*, edited by E. W. Tedlock, Jr. Copyright © 1961, 1964 by The Estate of Frieda Lawrence.

100 University of California Press and A. D. Peters & Co. Ltd:. For an excerpt from *World Within World: The Autobiography of Stephen Spender*. Copyright 1951 by Stephen Spender.

102 Harcourt Brace Jovanovich, Inc., The Hogarth Press Ltd., and Quentin Bell: For an excerpt from *Virginia Woolf: A Biography*, by Quentin Bell. Copyright © 1972 by Quentin Bell.

103 W. W. Norton & Co., Inc., and Russell & Volkening, Inc.: For an excerpt from *I Knew a Phoenix*, by May Sarton. Copyright 1954, © 1956, 1959 by May Sarton.

104 The Society of Authors as the literary representative of the Estate of James Stephens: For a quote by James Stephens from *James Joyce*, by Richard Ellmann. Originally appeared in "The James Joyce I Knew," *The Listener*, vol. XXXVI, October 24, 1946.

106 Mrs. Cyril Connolly: For an excerpt by Cyril Connolly from the Foreword to *Pictures and Conversations*, by Elizabeth Bowen.

107 University Press of Kansas: For an excerpt from *Sturge Moore and the Life of Art*, by Gwynn L. Frederick. Copyright 1951 by The University of Kansas Press.

108 Little, Brown and Company and David Higham Associates Ltd.: For an excerpt from *In My Own Time*, by John Lehmann. Published in 1969.

109 Harcourt Brace Jovanovich, Inc., The Hogarth Press Ltd., and the Literary Estate of Virginia Woolf: For an excerpt from *A Writer's Diary*, by Virginia Woolf. Copyright 1953, 1954 by Leonard Woolf.

A NOTE ON THE TYPE

The text of this book was set in a type face known as Garamond.
The design is based on letter forms
originally created by Claude Garamond (1510-1561).
Garamond was a pupil of Geoffroy Tory
and may have patterned his letter forms on Venetian models.
To this day, the type face that bears his name
is one of the most attractive used in book composition
and the passage of time has caused it to lose little
of its freshness or beauty.

Composed by Haddon Craftsmen, Scranton, Pa.
Printed by Halliday Lithographers, West Hanover, Mass.
Bound by The Book Press, Brattleboro, Vt.

Typography and binding design
by Camilla Filancia